TONY HIGGS

BREWIN BOOKS

First published by
Brewin Books Ltd, 56 Alcester Road,
Studley, Warwickshire B80 7LG in 2008
www.brewinbooks.com

Reprinted March 2009

ISBN: 978-1-85858-435-5

A Cataloguing in Publication Record
for this title is available from the British Library.

Typeset in Plantin
Printed in Great Britain by
Hobbs the Printers Ltd.

CONTENTS

INTRODUCTION

I first became aware of Monument Lane shed in the mid 1950s. My family had moved to Ladywood in 1954 and with an engine shed only a stone's throw away the noise and smoke quickly became a part of everyday life. However, my first real impression was gained one Sunday morning when my father called me into his bedroom and we watched as wagons were lifted up the side of the mechanical coaling plant and their contents tipped into the plant's bunker.

Before long I would look over the wall into the shed yard. We quickly grew to know the regulars, such as 44444, 47494, 58220 and the Class '5s' and we grew familiar with the sight of two Compounds, 40936 and 41168, stored out of harm's way in company with '4F' 44506.

At the same time there would be a procession of trains passing on the main line from Birmingham to Wolverhampton. Many were steam hauled, interspersed with some diesel multiple units. When we did see a main line diesel it would be one of the LMS types 10000 and 10001 or the former Southern Region units 10201/ 10202/10203.

To the young observer Monument Lane only appeared to be a small shed as the glamour engines of the London Midland Region were not allocated there. But small though it might have been, the shed had a vital part to play in keeping the Birmingham rail network moving. They were involved in some of the 2 hour expresses between Birmingham and London, kept a busy suburban service moving and played their part in the transportation of goods traffic. Monument Lane also became the first diesel shed in Birmingham and was, for a time, the largest diesel shed in the country.

It is now over 40 years since the shed closed but I hope that this account will provide some insight into the shed's operations, with new information on the early years and a feel for the responsibilities that fell to the men of Monument Lane.

ACKNOWLEDGEMENTS

This account could not have been compiled without a considerable amount of help from a number of people. From the Steam Locomotive Research Society my thanks are due to Richard Strange, Ben Brooksbank, Bill Rear, Ray Townsin, Ross Woollard and Chris Coates. Members of the London and North Western Society include Ted Talbot, whose father worked at Monument Lane in the 1930s and Harry Jack. In addition, Bob Essery, Ben Stone, Neville Simms, Mike Macleur, Norman Claydon and Jack Haddock willingly supplied information from their own material.

For the photographs I owe thanks to: Roger Carpenter, Alan Wycherley, Michael Mensing, Roger Shenton, Michael Whitehouse, John Edgington, David Johnson and Mark Norton, David Hanson and Richard Casserley for access to their father's collections, the Locomotive Club of Great Britain for use of the Kenn Nunn collection, Colin Stacey and the photographers of Initial Photographics, Rail Archive Stephenson, the Transport Treasury, the LNWR Society, Kidderminster Railway Museum, the Transport Treasury, Paul Chancellor and Jeremy Suter on behalf of the Gordon Coltas Trust for making their collections available to me. I am also grateful to Paul Bevand for preparing his superb drawings and for his company on what always seemed to be long and wet journeys returning from Kew.

For help with my researches I am indebted to staff at Birmingham Central Library, National Archives, the National Railway Museum, Walsall Local History Centre and Warwickshire County Records Office. Other sources have included *Trains Illustrated*, *The Railway Magazine*, *Railway Observer* and the *Journal of the Stephenson Locomotive Society*.

One of the most enjoyable aspects of preparing this book has been meeting the men of Monument Lane who have willingly offered their help and support. They were George Dixon (GD) who made me welcome in his home on many occasions, Brian Clarke (BC), who was a passport into his colleagues and who has never lost his willingness to answer my questions and to show his interest in my progress. The men with whom he put me in touch have all been similarly helpful. Frank Ward (FW) also shared his diaries and John Dean (JD) had records of duties in the 1950s. Many others willingly gave their time, namely Terry Smith (TS), 'Doc' Neale (RN), Les Riddle (LR), Alan Parker (AP), Bob Hardy, Stan Siverns, Brian Swanson (BS), Roy Judge, Tom Harrison and Derek Tyson. In addition, Charlie Bowyer and Dave Wakelin gave memories as visitors to the shed from other depots and Brian Blumfield shared memories of his father Vic, who was a top link driver. Some of the men that I met are sadly no longer with us, such as Howard Turvey, Reg Lewis (RL), Jack Williams and Cliff Wall (CW), all of whom played their part in assembling this account. A number have their specific memories included. Where they are not named in the text they can be identified by the initials shown here.

And finally, my thanks to my family for their support and encouragement at all times.

Monument Lane's Fairburn Tank loco 42674 is all set to pilot 'Patriot' 45539 *E C Trench* on the 2pm from New Street to Liverpool and Manchester on 10 January 1957. 42674 will come off at Dudley Port in order to work a freight train from Palethorpe's meat factory. *Michael Mensing.*

1

THE HISTORY OF THE SHED

THE EARLY YEARS

In the pre-grouping era of Britain's railways Monument Lane motive power depot was operated by the London and North Western Railway. However, its roots lay in the development of services between Birmingham New Street and Wolverhampton by the Birmingham, Wolverhampton and Stour Valley Railway Company, which the L&NWR eventually absorbed.

The Stour Valley Railway Company was by no means an early player in the development of the rail network in Birmingham. The first lines actually reached Birmingham in 1837 with the opening of the Grand Junction Railway's line from the north west of England. That route was followed by the London and Birmingham's line from Euston to Birmingham, which opened in stages during 1837 and 1838.

It was not until 1 July 1852 that passenger services were launched between Birmingham and Wolverhampton on the Stour Valley route, and it was that opening that would lead to the construction of Monument Lane's locomotive depot.

BIRMINGHAM'S FIRST LOCOMOTIVE DEPOTS

Both of the early railway companies established locomotive depots close to the centre of Birmingham. The London and Birmingham opened theirs at Curzon Street, with the Grand Junction doing so in nearby Vauxhall. When the two companies merged in 1846 to form the London and North Western Railway, Vauxhall fell within the Company's Northern Division and Curzon Street within the Southern Division.

It was March 1853 before moves began to erect a locomotive shed on the Stour Valley line, at a time when the London and North Western Railway was taking control of the route. Consequently, it was the Northern Division of the LNW Locomotive Committee that registered the need for the shed. The site was initially identified as 'The Crescent', the name of a local thoroughfare, and the depot was to be capable of holding 8 or 9 locomotives. The Committee approved the request, with a stipulation that tenders should be submitted in time for the next meeting in April. Clearly submitting a tender for railway work was not a complicated business in those days because several bids were available for the committee members to consider on 8 April, with costings ranging from £2795 to £3887. The figure of £2795 was deemed to be acceptable and the work was therefore awarded to A C Pauling. The name of the shed also became fixed as Monument Lane from that time.

Monument Lane engine shed was located in the Ladywood district of Birmingham and one contemporary writer felt bound to record the impact that the coming of the railway had on the area, observing that, 'Few districts of Birmingham have altered so thoroughly during the present reign as has that of Ladywood, but here and there in its seemingly endless labyrinth of blue bricked streets are still to be seen a few relics of the days when the site of the present London and North Western line, and other regions adjacent to St Vincent Street and Ryland Street, were gorgeous with apple blossom'.

Any remaining apple blossom would soon disappear in the vicinity of Monument Lane engine shed as construction work progressed, and soon the area had the ever present pall of smoke common to locomotive depots. By 1854, Birmingham Council's rating documentation shows the land adjacent to St Vincent Street and Sheepcote Lane to be occupied by an engine house, store room, a stationary engine house, over which was an iron cistern, a loading shed, coke store, warehouse and offices.

The engine shed was a modest construction, initially stabling twelve engines rather than the original nine that had been proposed. The building itself stood parallel to the down main line and consisted of three through roads. In addition, a line ran alongside the shed between the building and the main line. Access to the site was at the western or Wolverhampton end of the layout and the 42 foot turntable and coaling stage were located a little distance away from the shed buildings, beyond the St Vincent Street road bridge. The offices also formed part of the building and were located on the side of the shed away from the main line. They consisted of the Locomotive Superintendent's Office, a stores, an engine driver's room and the smithy's shop. Alongside the smithy's shop was a small area containing toilets, beyond which was a coking furnace. In addition, a small yard to stable locomotives existed alongside the building.

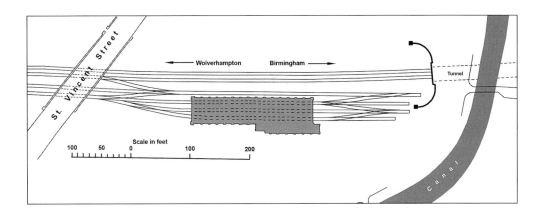

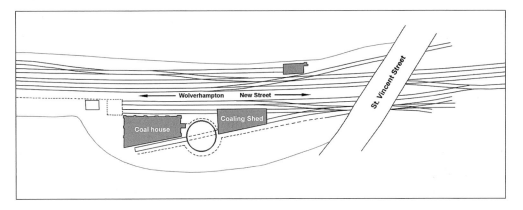

The original shed and separate coaling shed and turntable.

FURTHER EXPANSION

As the railway network developed still further, by 1855 there was a need to expand Curzon Street again. By then much of Curzon Street's passenger traffic had moved to New Street station; instead Curzon Street was growing in importance as a goods station. However, further expansion was hampered by the need to develop not only the locomotive depot but also the goods facilities, and there was insufficient land to do both.

There were also capacity issues at Vauxhall, so proposals were submitted in May 1856 to increase the allocation to 24 at Monument Lane. At first further changes were put on hold and it was overcrowding at Curzon Street that eventually forced the company to act. Thus, on Boxing Day 1857 the relevant committee met to consider how to address the problem. Following the discussions, the committee members agreed to enlarge the sheds at Vauxhall and Monument Lane so as to hold the engines housed at Curzon Street. The estimated cost was £7,500 and Mr Baker was asked to confer with the Locomotive Superintendents and prepare plans and obtain a tender accordingly.

Authority for the work at both Monument Lane and Vauxhall came on 10 February 1858. The LNW received ten tenders for the work, with approval going to Thomas Smith of Leicester. The total cost, including the improvements at Vauxhall, was £4,524 and twelve shillings (60p). Once again, success in gaining the contract was helped by the fact that the successful bidder submitted the lowest price.

Over the succeeding months the existing infrastructure at Monument Lane was re-decorated and minor repairs carried out, whilst materials for the new work arrived from London. Eventually, the new building was completed at an angle of around 45 degrees away from the old shed, itself just over five years old and which remained in use. The new building was referred to as the 'New Shed at Monument Lane', an identification which remained for many years. The new facilities provided six roads of 150 feet accommodation in addition to the three (of 200 feet) at the old shed. The New Shed also incorporated an additional block of offices, including a stores, mess room, fitters' shop, sand stores, and an extra toilet block. It has to be said, though, that there were few opportunities to provide a lavish layout. Bounded on two sides by local streets, on another by the Birmingham to Wolverhampton canal and on the fourth by the main line, the site lay in a tightly confined basin. That meant that there would never be a large allocation of engines at the shed and in fact numbers were often around 30,

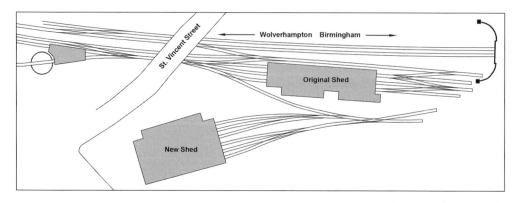

The shed layout in 1858.

rising for periods to just over 40. Nevertheless, Birmingham did not possess any engine sheds of a size comparable to Camden, Longsight in Manchester or Liverpool's Edge Hill and Monument Lane would play a key role in railway operations originating in the Birmingham area.

On 11 November 1858 Mr Baker reported that the shed at Monument Lane was ready for acceptance by the Locomotive Department. It therefore took its place within the Company's Northern Division. The move led to the closure of Curzon Street shed in 1859.

It appears that Monument Lane was allocated the depot code number 11 for a time, although it is not clear when it was last used. Later, following the closure of Vauxhall and the opening of Aston shed in 1884 – coded 10 – Monument Lane became a sub shed of Aston and was coded 10M.

The name of the shed is something of a puzzle, as the thoroughfare known as Monument Lane was sited over half a mile away from the shed buildings, which actually lay alongside St Vincent Street and Sheepcote Street. To further complicate the matter, the road bearing the name was changed to Monument Road in 1878 but the station and engine shed were never similarly altered.

On 30 December 1869, following a visit by the Chairman of the Company to the Birmingham area, it was recommended that three lines in the shed should be given over to the accommodation of carriages to help ease congestion at New Street, a move that was authorised on 6 January 1870. It was to prove a short term arrangement, as there were continuing problems at Vauxhall to the extent that the Company's Locomotive Superintendent John Ramsbottom found it necessary to transfer a considerable number of engines across Birmingham to Monument Lane. He therefore called upon Mr Bore to give up his portion of the shed devoted to carriages, a request that was approved on 11 March 1870.

The work falling to the depot began to gradually increase over the following twenty years as more lines were opened in the Birmingham area, including those to Sutton Coldfield, Harborne and then an extension beyond Sutton to Lichfield. Similar expansion occurred on the freight front as new yards opened and others were expanded along the Stour Valley line.

The extensions to the leafy suburbs of Harborne and Sutton would have provided some welcome relief from the dismal working conditions on the Stour Valley route. Captain J L Simmons, the Board of Trade Inspector inspecting the line when it first opened, described, 'The dense state of the atmosphere which frequently prevails and the vast number of furnaces and works with open fires and creating smoke adjacent to the railway which renders it very difficult to distinguish signals, especially red lights at night'.

Life at Monument Lane continued without any notable changes taking place until the mid 1880s, although there was a minor fire on 22 July 1884 affecting the roof of the New Shed. Fortunately the fire was discovered at an early stage by one of the firemen on duty and he extinguished the blaze by means of a hose pipe attached to the injector of an adjacent engine. The damage was estimated at around £50.

On 22 March 1884, following another of the Chairman's tours of inspection, it was proposed that an additional goods shed should be erected at Monument Lane and access improved to the site by means of an entrance from St Vincent Street. These changes affected the land occupied by the locomotive coal stage and turntable and those facilities were resited alongside the New Shed in 1886. Plans were also approved to build a new carriage shed near to Monument Lane station.

The layout at the shed was expanded slightly in 1915 with the provision of a seventh track adjacent to the New Shed. The additional track was laid using second hand materials, and came about in response to a need to improve access to the sand drying furnace, which was itself upgraded. The improved drying arrangements would meet the approval of the cleaners, who would climb under the roof space by the dryer during the cold winter months, as it was the warmest place in the shed!

During World War I women were often employed at engine sheds and Monument Lane was no exception. A company minute of 16 November 1916 noted that, 'owing to the engagement of females for engine cleaning and other work it is necessary that suitable lavatory accommodation and mess cabins be provided for female workers'. The cost of £120 for the work duly received approval.

MAJOR IMPROVEMENTS TAKE PLACE

During the 1930s the London Midland and Scottish Railway set out to enhance the layout of its shed yards to improve arrangements for the servicing of locomotives. Thus, on 25 May 1933 approval was given for new facilities at Monument Lane, including the provision of mechanical coaling and ash lift plants, both of which were available by 1934. They were built on the site of the original three road shed, which was demolished after a life of some fifty years.

The coaling plant was steel framed rather than of concrete design and of a type to be found at seven depots in total on the LMS. Wagons of coal were taken by the hoist to the top of the plant and tipped into a bunker of 75 ton capacity from which the fuel gravitated to a travelling skip at ground level. Unlike with many plants, the coaling road did not pass immediately beneath the structure, but to one side of it.

The ash plant was very much of standard LMS design of the period. The disposal men would remove the ashes from the engine ash pans onto the floor of the pit and it then became the ash pit men's job to shovel the ashes down the chute into the ash hoist skips. The skip was pulled up guide rails, using ropes, pulleys and counter weights and its contents tipped into a wagon which stood on the next road.

The disposal men had a mess room beneath the water tank and beyond the disposal men's room was the borehole which supplied all the water for the locos. The pumps and associated equipment for this were in the same building, as were pumps that supplied high pressure water for the lifts at New Street station.

There was room to accommodate the new facilities at the site, but they added to the cramped nature. One driver who visited regularly from another shed observed that, "Everything was squeezed – just room to get by here, get by there". Moreover, after passing under the St Vincent Street road bridge, drivers found themselves immediately in the shed yard, with the need to keep a careful lookout for other movements.

Under a reorganisation carried through in 1935 the shed was recoded 3E, placing it within a district that had Bescot as the lead shed. Further improvements included updated lighting in the shed and offices and a new turntable of 60 feet diameter was also installed; a water softening plant followed in 1938. The shed yard was also extended by the addition of three roads. They, together with the additional track laid in 1915, were at a slightly higher level than the existing shed yard and a rail separated those four tracks from the rest of the yard, leading the area to become known by the men as 'The Promenade'. In November 1938 approval was given for improved office accommodation and staff amenities, with the contract awarded to Edward Wood and Sons at a value of £2,365. At the same time the Brightside Foundry Engineering Company installed heating and hot water services at a cost of £342.

Given its size, the shed did not possess the equipment to carry out heavy repairs on locomotives. Where heavier repairs were required which did not necessitate a trip to the Works, engines were normally sent to Bescot, or

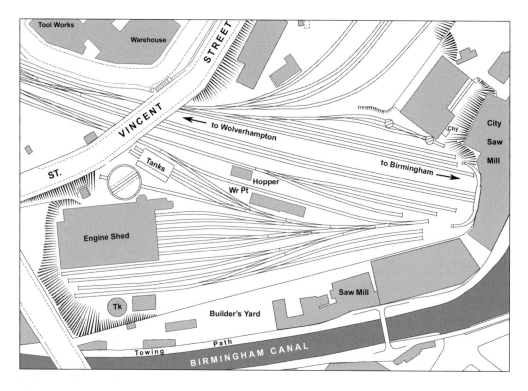

The final layout of the steam shed post 1939.

occasionally Aston. The Fitters' Room reflected this situation, possessing mainly a mix of hand tools, including large spanners stored on racks. Monument Lane did have its own breakdown carriage but no steam crane.

The improvements in the years prior to World War II were the last of any significance to take place at the steam shed. During the War the shed survived the major bombing campaigns which targeted the centre of Birmingham, although three incendiary devices did land near the shed, including one in Malthouse Sidings, opposite the original building, and one in Monument Lane Goods Yard, but damage to the structures was minimal. Women were also employed again at the shed during the war years.

In the aftermath of the War a problem of a different nature began to surface – a shortage of manpower. The war years left the railway infrastructure in a run down state but in the Birmingham area there were also problems with recruitment. Other industries could offer higher rates of pay and far better working hours, particularly the fast growing car industry. To illustrate the position, Les Riddle applied for a job with the Great Western Railway but was unsuccessful when only two out of fifteen applicants were accepted. Shortly afterwards he went to see the Shedmaster at Monument Lane and started work the following day! Such was the shortage of labour that one of the foremen, it is believed, would stand outside the nearby Winson Green prison on release days to try to boost recruitment.

As the 1950s progressed a derailment in one of the entrances to the shed damaged the front of the building and as a result part of the roof had to be cut back. With dieselisation on the horizon there was little prospect of investment in the steam facilities. However, one major development was yet to take place at Monument Lane.

THE DIESEL ERA

In 1954 some of the first signs of the British Railways' Modernisation Programme were appearing in the form of lightweight diesel multiple units. It was soon felt that the line from New Street to Lichfield would prove suitable for conversion to diesel operation and discussions moved on to the identification of a suitable location for cleaning, fuelling and servicing the units. At first two sites were proposed – Monument Lane and Four Oaks – but eventually Monument Lane emerged as the preferred single choice, especially as a particularly suitable location was available in the form of the Carriage Shed.

HISTORY OF THE CARRIAGE SHED

The origins of the Diesel Shed can be traced back to 1884 when approval was forthcoming for a Carriage Shed to be built on the up side of the Birmingham to Wolverhampton line, slightly to the north of Monument Lane station. Work was finally completed in 1886 and at that time one of the plumbers who was working on the water tank had an unnerving experience when he witnessed the engine of the 1.35pm from Wolverhampton separate from its train. He was powerless to act and a collision occurred in New Street station, happily without loss of life.

The new Carriage Shed consisted of six roads, three of which originally had pits. However, as railway carriages improved in terms of comfort, incorporating steam heating and electric lighting, they required additional servicing and the lack of pits on three of the roads meant that a considerable amount of shunting was often required to enable examinations to take place. Consequently, in 1905 it was agreed that pits would be installed on all roads. Arrangements were also

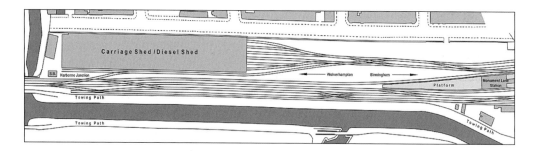

The Carriage Shed and Diesel Shed.

made to install carriage washing facilities in one span of the shed, all of which would, one day, make the site a suitable location for housing and servicing the new diesel units. Moreover, the shed was away from the steam depot, which meant that it was relatively free from the ever-present consequences of steam, smoke and soot which would have a detrimental effect on the railcar engines and general state of cleanliness.

Other alterations included the installation of fuelling points and a fuel tank, vacuum testing equipment and improvements to the drainage, although men who worked at the shed would question the extent of those 'improvements'. Arrangements were made for road access to the site, to allow for fuel deliveries in case of emergency. At the back of the shed, beneath the water tank, provision was made for an area for the fitters and the shed also had a small Foreman's office, in reality a partitioned area in the fitters' room.

There was also a need to widen the pits and the original intention to extend to 4ft 3 inches was overturned in favour of 4ft 4 inches, as the wider dimensions would allow for the servicing of electric stock in the future. Electric units were indeed introduced in the Birmingham area before the shed closed, but the tracks in the shed area were never 'wired up'.

As a number of Birmingham area suburban services remained steam hauled, carriage and wagon staff continued to have a presence at the Diesel Shed. In order to meet those needs, of the four carriage roads that sat alongside the two diesel maintenance roads, two were eventually designated for steam carriages and two for diesel. Road access to the site was from Cope Street. Altogether, the cost for alterations was budgeted at £18,800, enabling the building to become, for a short time at least, the largest diesel shed in the country.

THE DIESEL SHED OPENS

Before the service could be launched the crews had to be trained, so the first two-car unit arrived on 10 December, in the form of M79121 and M79642, and the practice runs began between Lichfield City and Four Oaks shortly afterwards. The new unit was immediately housed in the Carriage Shed and further sets arrived during January 1956. The training proceeded as required and the diesel service began on Monday 5th March 1956.

In the early days the DMUs were fuelled using a semi rotary pump, an extremely time consuming task. Basic maintenance was also carried out at the shed. One of the biggest jobs undertaken was the changing of final drives, which involved bringing the steam crane from Bescot to lift the railcar. That, though, was a job that took place at the former steam shed. The fitters could also test and set injectors and undertake gearbox changes. For more demanding jobs, such as engine changes, the units were sent to Bescot or Aston, usually accompanied by the fitters.

Units reached the shed by running past the building on the down main line and then setting back at Harborne Junction Signal Box into a siding alongside the shed; that siding then gave access to the shed yard. Units leaving the depot did so at the Monument Lane station end of the layout. The diesel shed did not receive a separate depot code, using the same 3E identification as the steam shed.

Although the diesels were slowly taking over, Monument Lane still had no diesel shunters at this stage. They had actually been present at other ex-LNW sheds in the area for some time – even as early as 1949 in the case of Aston – whilst Bescot and Walsall all had examples by 1953. At Monument Lane, though, the 1950s rolled on with steam in complete control of all of the trip work and shunting duties that fell to the shed.

Following a re-organisation of Birmingham Motive Power Districts, the shed was recoded 21E from 20 June 1960, placing it in the Saltley District. In January 1961 the shed gained some temporary additional work following a fire which damaged Aston No 1 Signalbox. One of the responsibilities of the signalbox was to control access to Aston shed, so while repairs were carried out some additional engines were sent to Monument Lane for servicing.

During the early months of 1961 rumours began to circulate that the shed would close at the start of the Summer Timetable. That rumour proved to be unfounded and an intake of seven 'Black 5s' demonstrated that the shed would again play its part in supporting the additional workings during the Summer months.

Before steam operations were officially withdrawn one last major incident occurred. During the afternoon of 31 December 1961, a 'B1' leaving the shed overshot a signal and demolished Sheepcote Lane signalbox. Signalman Harold Dix was on duty at the time and fortunately escaped serious injury. However, the immediate consequences were severe, affecting access into and out of the shed and disrupting services on the main line. The signalbox was too seriously damaged to be repaired and was replaced by a more modern structure on the same site.

Shortly afterwards the shed officially closed to steam with effect from 10 February 1962. Some steam locomotives from other sheds continued to arrive for basic servicing but the withdrawal of coaling facilities limited the extent of that servicing. However, the ongoing existence of the diesel shed meant that many of the men could remain at Monument Lane. Moreover, they continued to work on steam locomotives from other sheds as well as main line diesels and the steam shed continued to be used as the signing on point.

One further change was to take place in September 1963, when the shed was recoded 2H, placing it in the Tyseley district. Thus in its time Monument Lane became a sub-shed to depots built by the London and North Western, Midland and Great Western Railways. During the 1960s plans progressed for electrification of lines in the Birmingham area and it became clear that a new depot for the units would be built at nearby Soho. Monument Lane therefore finally closed during the first week of March 1967 and the men were transferred to New Street.

The sheds remained unused for a short time but the steam shed was demolished in 1968. The date of demolition of the diesel shed is not known but both sites remained derelict for a number of years. Eventually the steam shed site became part of the National Indoor Arena complex, where a car park takes up much of the shed site. The diesel shed site, though, still remained undeveloped in 2008.

THE OUTSTATIONS – TIPTON AND ALBION

Monument Lane had responsibility for two locations away from the main site, at Tipton and Albion, both of which were on the Stour Valley line.

Tipton

Tipton had the more substantial facilities of the two, possessing a small, one road engine shed. LNW company minutes show that proposals were approved in 1884 to station a shunting engine at Tipton to work alongside the horses and that a shed should be provided to house the locomotive. That move led to redundancies for four of the horses!

The shed was situated on the down side of the main line, squeezed up against a wall separating it from a canal towpath. The provision of the shed meant that a locomotive could remain at Tipton throughout the week. It therefore left the main shed on Monday morning, worked by Monument Lane men, and was remanned at Tipton by local men. It then remained at Tipton until the local men worked it back on Saturday evening.

The shed had its own pit and a water tank and engines were coaled by hand from a truck that was taken down to one of the two lines in the basin. Ash from the engine would be dumped alongside the shed road and taken away by platelayers at regular intervals.

There would be a break from shunting at about one o'clock when the engine was stabled by the coal wagon and the fireman was left in charge to coal the engine. Coaling also took place at night from a coal stage near the shed. At one time the night fireman was expected to empty the wagon, for which he was paid overtime.

The shed was manned by two drivers and three firemen, with the firemen working three shifts and the drivers two. The driver on days would finish at around 1.30pm and the afternoon driver would book on at 2 o'clock. He then worked a complete day, sometimes with overtime, before he left the engine on the shed. The firemen worked three eight hour shifts and the night shift fireman had to clean the engine and maintain steam.

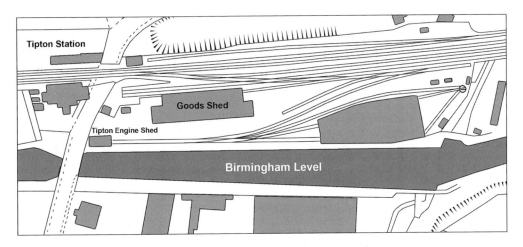

Tipton Engine Shed.

The locomotive was a hand braked saddle tank when George Crumpton arrived as a fireman in 1919 but before World War II life on the footplate was made considerably easier by the arrival of Midland Class '1' tank engines. They were followed during World War II by ex LNW 1F 'Box Tanks', which included 27480 and 27484 in the 1940s. Most common during the shed's latter days were 0-6-2 'Coal Tanks' and 'Watford Tanks'.

The shed closed around 1953, leading to the redundancy of George Crumpton, who transferred to Bescot. However, driver Len Neville remained along with firemen Alan Parker and Les Porter. Len Neville retired around 1957 and he was replaced by Alan Whitehouse.

After the shed closed, Monument Lane men would bring the engine to Tipton on a daily basis.

Albion

Similar arrangements applied at Albion, except that there was no shed to house the locomotive. As with Tipton the engine left Monument Lane on Monday morning and returned during Saturday evening. Apart from the lack of a shed it was not until 1904 that the site even had a water column. Instead, shunting engines had to go to Dudley Port for water. The site also had an engine pit and, as with Tipton, the practice of outstationing an engine ended in 1953.

Midland Railway Class '2' 0-6-0s were the normal engines used after their arrival at Monument Lane shed in the 1930s. The drivers over the years included Jimmy Asbury, Billy Bear and Billy Disley. Cliff Wall recalled that Jimmy Asbury's fireman was named Knight and he was nearly as old as his driver because he was an ex Midland man and was a 'Permanent Fireman', a grade used by the Midland Railway. In later years Sam Adams was the fireman.

THE SHED'S LINKS

Information on the shed's links is a little uncertain, not least since it has not been possible to find any evidence of the arrangements in the earlier years of the shed's existence. Other complications also exist and the position changed with the coming of the diesels.

However, it has been possible to identify a reasonably clear picture for some of the time. Broadly speaking the link structure for most of the men in the days of steam, beginning with the top link was:

Link Number and Local Identification	Areas covered
1A	London & Manchester
1B	London and Liverpool
2 ('Big Tank' or 'Cathedral Link') (Mainly passenger)	Lichfield, Stafford, Rugeley, Walsall, Coventry, Rugby, Leamington
No 3 ('Gadget') Link (Freight)	Harborne, Soho Pool, Bescot trips, Stechford, Four Oaks
Spare Link	
Shunting Link	Monument Lane, Soho, Spon Lane, Oldbury
Disposal Link	

Two additional links – and possibly three – also existed which, strictly speaking, were outside the normal lines of progression. The simplest to explain were the residential and the bank links. The residential covered Tipton and Albion and, unless they chose otherwise, men remained at those locations. George Crumpton, for example, took up one of the posts of fireman at Tipton in 1919 and became a driver in 1939 on the retirement of one of the drivers at Tipton.

The bank link covered the New Street pilot engines at the north end of the station and was open to top link drivers who wished to 'retire' from the main line. They could therefore apply for a vacancy in that link when one arose. The 'Cathedral Link' was the name given to Number 2 link as many of the duties were to Lichfield. However, that may have been a name bestowed on Number 2 link in later years, as Cliff Wall, who worked at the shed from the 1930s, recalled that it was a link of four jobs reserved for men who did not wish to progress to the main line links but which presumably included Lichfield as a main destination. The nickname 'Gadget Link' is the reference to the fact that many of the duties – usually shunting turns – were carried out by 'Coal Tanks', which were referred to locally as 'Gadgets'.

The arrival of diesel multiple units brought about a major change to the link structure. The shunting and spare links remained, but at which point the routes split, with numbers 4 and 3 links designated for DMUs and links 2, 1B and 1A reserved for steam turns.

2

MAIN LINE WORKINGS

Monument Lane's regular long distance main line workings revolved primarily around services between Birmingham and London, Liverpool and Manchester. They would also work shorter distance services on the same routes, such as to Crewe and Rugby. In addition, Summer workings and excursions took the men further afield, as the depot always had a number of drivers who signed the road to Blackpool, Rhyl and Llandudno.

The arrival of diesels and the work to prepare for electrification of the lines to London and the north west impacted significantly on the shed's main line workings, so it is best to examine them before and after the diesels arrived.

BEFORE THE DIESELS
London
Monument Lane men regularly worked to London but responsibility for hauling the faster services often fell to Bushbury and Camden. In 1900, for example, William Woods from Monument Lane recalled that he was one of three drivers from Birmingham chosen to work the faster trains. However, in 1905, with the introduction of two hour expresses from Birmingham to the capital, Birmingham men lost the majority of the workings. LNW Locomotive Committee minutes record that, 'To carry out the accelerated service between Euston and Birmingham from 1 March next, and avoid changing engines at New Street, they will run through to Wolverhampton and be stabled at Bushbury'. Monument Lane men were not totally excluded though, as William Woods recalled that he was also involved on those services.

The position fluctuated again around the time of World War I but by the 1930s Bushbury and Camden were once again in the ascendancy. Nevertheless, a few London workings did remain with Monument Lane, although they were more usually trains that were booked to run via Northampton, such as the 10.10am from Birmingham to Euston in the 1930s, or relief services.

A similar trend continued after World War II, although in the early post war years timings were slower as the railways struggled to recover from the effects of the hostilities.

In the mid to late 1940s we used to have a Compound on the 9.35pm ex Euston on Saturday nights. The war was just finished and most locos were in a poor state. In addition, we were nearly always overloaded so we used to have a really rough trip; this trip was always known as 'Battle of Britain Night'. (CW).

The 9.35 did provide the men with some light entertainment in the early stages of the journey.

There used to be one of the local electric trains leave Euston at 9.35, first stop Watford. At 9.35 we were fast line and he used to go down the subway. He'd show us a clean pair of heels but as soon as we got the other side of Willesden he'd have his controller flat out and we'd go flying by. (GD).

On Mondays and Fridays we worked the 2.20pm, which was a relief to the 2.35pm up from Wolverhampton. We had the 11.10 parcels at night and that was a booking off job – in the 1940s we stayed there all day Monday until 9.35 at night. Another regular London working was the 5pm, which ran from Tuesdays to Fridays via Northampton. (GD).

In 1953 two hour expresses were re-introduced between Birmingham and London. Although those workings again fell to Bushbury and Camden, the heavier trains would require assistance, usually on Fridays and Saturdays. That work fell to Monument Lane, who often used their Compounds, 40933, 40936 and 41090. As a result, the Monument Lane men – and their Compounds – were involved in some of the fastest steam hauled trains on the London Midland Region, although the price to pay was two hours of intense noise and rattling on an engine which by then was better suited to sedate secondary duties. Not all London trips were on pilot engines, though.

On Friday afternoons Stoke on Trent men used to work from Stoke to Rugeley. Then, up the bank from Rugeley they would stop at Brindley Heath, where they would pick up all the RAF men going home on leave, before working into New Street via Walsall and Soho Road. We used to relieve them and we would work forward as the 2.20pm, which was a relief to the 2.30pm to London, with their engine. I recall 45257 on this working. (BC).

The Brindley Heath working did not always enjoy such motive power; during the late 1940s Reg Lewis and Jack Williams recalled that it was often a Midland '2P' 4-4-0.

Other workings during the mid to later 1950s were the 4.30pm to Euston on Sundays, booked at one time for a Bushbury 'Jubilee', and the 5.20pm to Euston, worked by a Monument Lane Class '5'. In addition, the men assisted the 08.30am from New Street to Euston before returning in the evening by assisting the 'Midlander' to New Street.

With the 8.30 we used to have a 'Black 5'. In would roll the train from Wolverhampton – the 7.55am. We would hook on, then it was Coventry and right away into London. They were some of the fastest timed trains in the country. On Mondays to Fridays you were timed from Coventry to London 94 miles in 94 minutes. (BC).

The men would also be expected to know the variations in route that might occur. That included signing the road for the two routes to Northampton, either directly via Roade or from Blisworth. Other diversions could occur, too.

One Sunday, when working the 4.50pm to Euston, due to repairs in Kilsby tunnel, we were diverted via Leamington, then the Rugby line to Marton Junction, then via Napton and Daventry to Weedon, then back onto the main line. (CW).

In terms of motive power for the London workings, after the period when the shed had its 'Newtons' and 'Jumbos' the most likely power would be 'Precursor' 4-4-0s, 'George V' 4-4-0s, 'Experiment' 4-6-0s or 'Prince of Wales' 4-6-0s. Compound 4-4-0s also played a major role following their introduction at the shed in 1925, although Stanier Class '5s' were the preferred choice if available from the late 1930s onwards.

MANCHESTER

From the earliest days Monument Lane men worked through to Manchester, usually via Crewe rather than Stoke. As was the practice at the time, some trains left New Street bound for both Manchester and Liverpool and were divided at Crewe. In the post nationalisation period the depot had two regular express return workings to Manchester, leaving New Street at 7.10am and 12.10pm.

The 7.10am was Wolverhampton, Stafford, Crewe, Stockport and Manchester – Mayfield in those days. They fetched the coaches off us and we went on to the table. To return we hooked onto the local 11.10am to Crewe, where we hooked off and went onto the North shed to book off. We then booked on at 11.25 at night to work the 12.05am parcels – 24 vans to New Street. (RL).

We approached New Street round the city via Bescot. Then, when we had unloaded, we swapped footplates with the men off the North pilot on the LNW side, which was manned by Monument Lane men. We would be relieved at 4am.

On Saturday nights there was a different arrangement. We would work the mail vans from Crewe as usual to New Street. After it was unloaded we'd take the coaches to Vauxhall carriage sidings, take the engine onto Aston shed and then be expected to make our own way back to Monument Lane. That normally meant catching a tram or bus to the shed. (GD).

After 1950 the men returned from Manchester on a different service.

The morning turn was a lodging turn. We booked on at 4.30, went light engine to Vauxhall carriage shed for our train, the 7.10am New Street to Manchester London Road, then worked back to Crewe with the 12.15pm to Plymouth. (FW).

Before the railcars came the 12.10 was worked by a Monument Lane engine, Engine Turn No 1, which left the shed at 6.30 to the carriage shed, where it was used for shunting until it was time to take the stock for the 12.10am via Soho and Aston into New Street. It was relieved there by the second set of men, who worked to Manchester and back. 44942 was the engine we used on this job wherever possible because it had a rocker grate and hopper ashpan, which made it easier for the men cleaning the fire during the turn around at Manchester. (JD).

On arrival at London Road station we turned the engine, cleaned the fire and pulled the coal forward. We left there at 4.30pm, calling at Stockport, then Wolverhampton and New Street. We only had five coaches on this train. (FW).

The shed also worked the 9.35am to Manchester on Sundays, coming off at Stafford and occasionally there would be a working via Stoke.

I worked to Manchester via Stoke as a fireman when I went with Dick Challener. We walked to Saltley, to Landor St Jc, where we relieved a train that had come from Bournemouth, I believe with a 'Black 5'. We worked via the Sutton Park line, Wolverhampton, Stafford and then we went across the Potteries and we were relieved at Stockport. (BC).

LIVERPOOL

Liverpool workings were also a feature of services from the shed in the 19th Century, as Ebenezer Clarke recalled firing to Merseyside in the 1890s.

In the post World War II era there was one daily Monument Lane timetabled service, which set off for Merseyside from New Street at 9.10am. The return duty involved an overnight stop at Crewe for the men. The engine was used initially on the 2.50am parcels to Leamington, returning to New Street on the 7.55am local service from Leamington to New Street.

We would take the engine onto the shed at Warwick, get the fire ready and work back to New Street. It was an all stations job with ten coaches on so you can imagine what state the fire was in by the time that we were relieved by our own men to work on to Liverpool. (GD).

When we got to Liverpool we would stand in the station until they fetched the coaches off us. We would bank him up to Rainbow and go over the 'grid' and on to Edge Hill. The 'grid' was a triangle for turning. Then we coaled her, did the fire, filled her up and worked back to Crewe where we were relieved and booked off. We came back the next morning on the 5.40am to Birmingham, took the empty coaches to Vauxhall then went round the city and dropped her on the shed. She then went off on the 12.10pm to Manchester. (RL).

Once, when we worked through to Liverpool, we were given the last 'Claughton', 6004, for a local working back to Crewe. (GD).

The Manchester and Liverpool services used 'Jumbos' in the later Victorian era, followed by 'Precursors', 'Prince of Wales' and 'George Vs'. From the mid 1920s Compounds played a part, followed by Stanier Class '5s', although Compounds would still work through to Manchester after World War II. From the mid 1950s both Liverpool and Manchester services were booked to locomotives from other sheds, such as 'Royal Scots', 'Jubilees', Class '5s' – including the Caprotti variety from Longsight shed – and BR Standard Class '5s' in the 73xxx series from Shrewsbury shed. Monument Lane engines did return to the service at times in 1960.

RUGBY, STAFFORD & CREWE

Other main line turns took Monument Lane men to Rugby, Stafford and Crewe. Some of the Rugby workings then proceeded to the Eastern Region via Market Harborough, such as with the 8.45am and the 3.58pm. The latter train was known locally as 'The Continental'.

In addition, when working the 5.20pm from Euston to Rugby via Northampton the men would then take the engine on the shed at Rugby and return to the station to relieve the 7.00pm from Euston, taking it to New Street.

Later, on Saturday afternoons, we used to work to Rugby then across the branch to Peterborough, where we would book off. It was a Yarmouth train and the Eastern Region took over. We went onto the shed, turned the engine then we used to work back to Rugby on a local into one of the bays where they fetched the coaches off us and we ran light engine to Monument Lane. (BC).

SUMMER SATURDAYS AND EXCURSION TRAFFIC

For many years the depot was responsible for working Summer Saturday trains to Lancashire and North Wales. In the 1890s one such working was a Saturday evening service to Llandudno, which returned on Monday morning and was known as the 'Husbands' Train'.

By that time the railways had an important part to play in transporting people simply for pleasure. For the August Bank Holiday weekend of 1886, for example, Monument Lane men would help to transport thousands of people from the West Midlands to popular local spots, as well as the coastal resorts. The LNW reported that 16,000 locals booked on the Friday and Saturday for excursions to Blackpool and the North Wales coast and a further 10,000 travelled on the Sunday. Just over 2,000 booked to Blackpool alone on the Monday, despite the fact that it was a rainy day. Locally there were 2,700 combined bookings to Coventry, Kenilworth and Leamington, with 900 bookings for Sutton Coldfield.

From the late 1940s there were three regular timetabled workings involving Monument Lane men and engines. They were the 8.35am Smethwick to Llandudno, the 9.00am New Street to Blackpool and the 9.20am New Street to Morecambe. The locomotive to Blackpool returned on the 3.40pm to New Street – sometimes extending to Walsall – and the Llandudno service returned as the 2.50pm to New Street. The locomotive to Morecambe came off the train at Crewe.

The men also worked Summer extras between the West Midlands and the East and South coasts of England, although they would be relieved or take over en route. In the case of East coast trains Monument Lane men usually worked no further than Rugby – trains would then proceed via Market Harborough; for trains to or from the Southern Region they would work to or from the Willesden area.

During the late Victorian era many of the workings were frequently powered by 0-6-0 goods locomotives. In later years 'Precursors', 'George V' or 'Prince of Wales' locos played a more prominent part, such as when 5707 *Hampden* was observed at Colwyn Bay in the summer of 1932. Finally they were the preserve of the Compounds or Stanier Class '5s'.

SPECIALS

Monument Lane men worked a range of Specials, such as holiday extras, trains for sporting events, company outings, entertainment events or railtours.

One early example was back in 1895, when the FA Cup Final involved Aston Villa and West Bromwich Albion, and Monument Lane played its part in conveying many thousands of supporters to the capital for the game at Crystal Palace.

Grand National day also generated many Specials. In the early 1930s, for example, the shed's 'Prince of Wales' engines were reported working extra trains to Aintree on Grand National day, usually piloted by a Central Division loco for the last stages of the journey and there was a similar call on Monument Lane on Cup Final days.

There were also company specials, including those for the Co-op, Joseph Lucas, and Marsh and Baxter, often to North Wales and the Lancashire seaside resorts.

I had the annual Co-op outing twice to Rhyl. We picked up empty coaches from Vauxhall, with ten on, usually for an 8 o'clock start. It was a continuous duty where you'd work it through, book off and bring it back. Those jobs usually fell to men in the Special Link but if they didn't know the route then they would take men out of the Top Link or the Liverpool Link. Sometimes we used to get an Aston engine and I've got less than pleasant memories of a 'Crab' we had. (GD).

In the summer we had a train from London for the British Industries Fair, which the Cockneys would bring down. Saltley men would work it out to Castle Bromwich. Sometimes there were even Fowler Class '4' tanks on those trains, hauling 10 coaches; we would take it back to Euston. The last time that I worked it we had Falkland Islands *on it when she was a Camden engine. The engine would come onto Monument Lane and, of course, it had to be cleaned and polished up. (GD).*

By the mid 1950s, though, diesel multiple began to take over the BIF event.

Talking of Special workings, we used to take a train to Oundle for the start of term time at the school. I fired on that working from Birmingham on two occasions with a Compound, once with 1172. From Northampton we had a Northampton driver as pilot. Then we ran around the coaches at Oundle and brought them back to Northampton. From there we hooked on to a Wolverhampton express to get the engine back.

We also worked the 'Monkey Specials', which started back from Rugby or Coventry, and they were taken over at New Street for Bristol Zoo. (GD).

Left: The London and North Western Railway entrance plate to the shed still in place, despite its pre grouping origins, on 4 June 1950! *F A Wycherley*. Right: Amongst the earliest locomotives to arrive at Monument Lane were four Trevithwick single wheelers and this photograph is of a member of the class, 365 *Vesta*, which was introduced in 1855, and is believed to be in the shed yard at Monument Lane. *LNWR Society Collection/LNWRS 1994.*

The early goods engines at the shed included LNWR 0-4-2 number 601 (1906 from 1874), photographed around 1865. The locomotive has passed under the St Vincent Street bridge to reach the coal stage and turntable. Note the steps in the background which link Sheepcote Lane to St Vincent Street. They can still be climbed today. *Kidderminster Railway Museum.*

LNWR 'Old Crewe' 2-4-0 with a large firebox, number 337, is seen outside the original shed around the 1870s. The water tank dominates the background *R F Bleasdale courtesy Manchester Model Club/Kidderminster Railway Museum.*

LNWR Ramsbottom built 'Newton' 2-4-0 1525 *Abercrombie* stands in the shed yard on an unknown date. Built in 1866, the engine was scrapped in 1891. In the background is the Malthouse. *R F Bleasdale courtesy Manchester Model Club/Kidderminster Railway Museum.*

LNWR Ramsbottom built 'Newton' 2-4-0 1523 *Marlborough*. Built in 1866 this is seen in early Webb condition chimney, black livery and slotted splashers. *R F Bleasdale courtesy Manchester Model Club/Kidderminster Railway Museum.*

LNWR Sharp Stewart 'Large Bloomer' built in 1853 (formerly numbered 294) 2-2-2 894 *Trentham*. Seen with a Crewe DX boiler, Webb cab and black livery. The photograph was taken in 1872 and the engine scrapped in 1883. *R F Bleasdale courtesy Manchester Model Club/ Kidderminster Railway Museum.*

'Samson' Class 2-4-0 2158 *Serpent* was introduced in 1874 and is alongside the entrance to the original shed. *LNWR Society Collection.*

2-4-0 2250 stands in the shed yard. This class of locomotive was first introduced in 1876 and Monument Lane used it on local passenger workings. *LNWR Society Collection.*

An aerial view of the shed (to the top right) in the 1920s and the surrounding area. *Reproduced with permission of Birmingham Libraries and Archives.*

The six roads of the 'New Shed' are all clearly visible in September 1936. On the far right is the old coaling stage and the track between the two telegraph poles leads to the turntable. New offices would be built on the right hand side of the shed within two years. *W Potter/ Kidderminster Railway Museum.*

'Claughtons' were occasional visitors to Monument Lane and here is Rugby's 5964 *Patriot*, so named in memory of the LNWR employees who died in the World War I. In the background is the original shed, now near the end of its existence. *Rail Archive Stephenson*.

Unnamed 'Prince of Wales' 5711 stands alongside the original shed on 21 June 1931. *L W Perkins/F A Wycherley Collection*.

In 1934 a major renewal programme took place at the shed. The original three road building was demolished and a new mechanical coaling plant provided together with a new ash plant. 'Coal Tank' 7742 is at the shed on 23 September 1934 and the coaling plant is clearly in its final stages of construction. *L W Perkins/F A Wycherley Collection.*

It is 26 May 1935 and unnamed Patriot 5518 is on the ash pit at Monument Lane. The ash pit equipment is a recent improvement at the shed *L W Perkins/F A Wycherley Collection.*

Unnamed 'Patriot' 5551 is tucked inside the old coaling stage on 18 January 1948. Presumably the mechanical plant was out of action on this date, leading to some hard work for the shed labourers. 5551 is a Crewe North engine. *L W Perkins/F A Wycherley Collection.*

'Watford Tank' 46900 stands over one of the pits outside the shed during the early 1950s. The water tank is receiving some attention in the background and the shed entrance to the right provides evidence that the building once had doors. *Howard Turvey.*

Ex LNW 4-4-2 tank 6821 is stabled alongside the shed in the mid 1930s. By now the original shed building has been demolished and the new coaling and ash plants are in the background. 6821 was withdrawn at Monument Lane during week ending 12 December 1936. *C R Gordon Stuart/Rail Archive Stephenson.*

Longsight Compound 41166 stands alongside the shed on 3 July 1948. The locomotive has been coaled in preparation for its next working but is facing in the wrong direction for an immediate return to its home depot. It is therefore possible that the engine is ready to work the 5.8pm to Leamington, which fell to a Longsight locomotive at this time. Within months 41166 would transfer to Monument Lane. *H C Casserley.*

A definite rarity at Monument Lane, 0-4-0T 47184 is on shed circa 1950. This engine never appeared on Monument Lane's allocation lists so it is not possible to be certain about its presence at the shed but it may be as a result of a loan spell to M&B to cover a loco shortage at the company's Cape Hill sidings. *Howard Turvey.*

Class '4F' 44514 and 'Black 5' 45390 are stabled alongside the shed during the early 1950s. 45390 came to the shed in 1950 and left during week ending 10 March 1956, meaning that it stayed at 3E longer than any other 'Black 5'. It lasted until the end of steam on 'BR', hauling one of the railtours on the penultimate weekend. 44514 came in 1942 and remained at the shed until it closed to steam in February 1962. *Howard Turvey.*

The shed received six Johnson '2F' 0-6-0s in 1932 and from that time there was always a locomotive of that class present virtually until closure to steam. 58185 was a later arrival, transferring from Aston during week ending 26 January 1952 and it was the last member of the class to leave, officially transferring to Bescot during week ending 30 December 1961. It is seen here in the shed yard around 1957/58. *R S Carpenter Collection.*

Fairburn tank 42267 has just left the tunnel to the north of New Street station in the early 1950s and is climbing past the shed on its way to the carriage sidings with an empty stock working. The photograph shows how close the shed yard lay to the Stour Valley main line. *Joe Moss/R Carpenter Collection.*

Access to the shed was controlled by Sheepcote Lane Signal Box, seen in the distance in this view. Stafford Fowler tank 42389 stands in the siding close to the signalbox on a grey November day in 1958. Sheepcote Lane box was demolished by a 'B1' which overshot a signal in December 1961 and a new structure had to be provided. Monument Lane Goods shed dominates the scene. *Roger Shenton.*

Longsight 'Jubilee' 45631 *Tanganyika* moves along the shed yard after coaling and ash disposal on 4 August 1960. Alongside is '2P' 4-4-0 40692 which, although a Bescot engine, was stored at Monument Lane for a period. *F A Wycherley.*

Longsight's Class '5' 44687 on shed on 4 August 1960. This was one of two Class '5s' introduced after nationalisation with Caprotti valve gear and Skefko roller bearings. The other example, 44686, actually spent a short period at Monument Lane earlier in 1960. *F A Wycherley*.

The shed lost its final named locomotive as long ago as 1936 when Prince of Wales 25673 *Lusitania* moved away. In the last year of its Monument Lane career *Lusitania* has arrived at Leamington on a local working. *Gordon Coltas*.

When officialdom saw fit to send no named locomotives to Monument Lane the men took matters into their own hands and named one of the 'Coal Tanks', 58928, *Chipper* after a cartoon dog which appeared in a local newspaper. *Chipper* is shown taking a breather between duties as one of the New Street pilots on 1 August 1950. *T J Edgington*.

'Coal Tank' 58903 stands in the shed yard in 1954. Judging by its state of cleanliness it has been prepared to work two railtours which took place to mark the centenary of Birmingham New Street station on 1st and 2nd June 1954. At this time 58903 was the last ex LNW locomotive to be allocated to the shed and it would be withdrawn shortly afterwards. *R Butterfield/Initial Photographics*.

Shed 'roads' 7 to 10 were later additions and separated from the rest of the yard by a metal railing. They were known locally as 'The Promenade' and in the early 1950s they house '4Fs' 44361, 44490, Compound 40936, with its high sided tender, and a 2-6-4 tank. The water softening plant is in the background. *Joe Moss/Courtesy R Carpenter.*

Ex LNW Saddle tanks were to be found at the shed for many years. At one time on station pilot duties at New Street, they ended their days outstationed at Tipton shed. The last example was 27480, which left Monument Lane during the week ending 23 November 1946 in order to act as a Crewe Works shunter. It is seen here at Crewe Works in May 1948, still bearing its 3E shedplate. *Ben Brooksbank/Initial Photographics.*

Monument Lane controlled two outstations, the most substantial of which was Tipton, which had a one road engine shed, albeit large enough only for a tank engine. This view shows the shed in the 1930s with a locomotive tucked inside. *W A Camwell/R Carpenter Collection.*

Albion was the other outstation. There was no engine shed here and so tender engines could be used. Ex Midland Railway '2F' 0-6-0 58286 is accompanied by driver Reg Lewis (second from left) in 1955.

Main line work also took place during the area's Summer holiday fortnight, with men and engines working the 'City of Birmingham Holiday Express' specials to a variety of locations such as Blackpool and Alton Towers.

For the City of Birmingham Holiday expresses they'd polish up an engine and keep it on the job for a week. (BC).

Troop Specials during wartime also occurred.

We booked on one evening and then went light engine to Park Sidings (Soho). After picking up a train of empty coaches we proceeded via Soho Road, Bescot, Bushbury and Stafford to Salop where we hooked off and a Western man attached. We turned round the angle and attached to a troop train which had come in from Wales, then worked forward via Stafford, the Trent Valley line, Rugby, then to Mitre Bridge, where a Southern Railway loco and men worked forward to the South Coast. (CW).

On numerous occasions Monument Lane men were entrusted with Royal Train Duties. In the 1920s William Woods was in charge of a train carrying members of three Royal Families when he transported the Kings of Belgium, Portugal and Spain on their way to a wedding. On another occasion, on November 3rd 1955, two sets of men were called on when they were in charge of 'Black 5s' 45495 and 44906, both from 'foreign' sheds. Initially the men worked the empty stock from Kings Norton to Stechford, where the Royal party joined the train for the journey to Euston. Driver Charlie Sandells and fireman Johnny Cox took over the train engine and driver Vic Blumfield and fireman Roy Judge were on the footplate of the leading engine.

Roy Judge recalls that the working was the first occasion involving a Royal Train where a telephone was available on the footplate, enabling the Inspector who normally rode 'up front' to remain in the first carriage. The telephone was housed on the 'shelf' normally used for fire irons and spare lamps and had to be used underneath a cloth, like an old fashioned camera. It was tested successfully at Kings Norton and not required during the journey, although Roy believes it would not have been possible to hear the speaker above the usual noise on the footplate!

Royalty were late arriving at Stechford, so there was a 20 minute late start but time was made up and they were in Euston just over five minutes late. We had the engines for about a week beforehand and they were cleaned, polished and prepared by Monument Lane staff and I remember Jack Middleton's painting skills being used to good effect on those two engines. (JD).

It is also believed that Monument Lane men once worked a train conveying Winston Churchill.

AFTER THE DIESELS

Although diesel multiple units had taken over a number of suburban workings, the shed continued to operate a range of steam services, including some on local journeys. As far as main line services were concerned, it was business as usual, even though the shed initially lost its Class '5s' when the diesel multiple units began to operate. As a result the shed used locomotives from other depots when working to Manchester and Liverpool.

Monument Lane men also began to work on main line diesels, notably the two LMS English Electric prototypes 10000 and 10001 and the trio originally working on the Southern Region, 10201, 10202 and 10203. The diesels worked services between Birmingham and London, such as on 12 July 1957, when 10201 worked the 6.45pm from Euston to Wolverhampton and 12 August, when 10001 was at the head of the 10.40pm parcels service from Birmingham to London. Just to show that things weren't changing too dramatically in 1957, Compound 40936 piloted the 4.30pm from Euston on 2 September of that year!

Electrification was also planned, which meant that engineering work would take place over long stretches of the routes covered by Monument Lane engines. The first real impact on Birmingham came in November 1959, when many of the London Midland Region Birmingham to London expresses disappeared from the timetable in preparation for electrification. Even so, despite the reduction in London services, some workings still fell to Monument Lane. One such was to pilot the 6.15pm Euston to Crewe as far as Coventry. There, two coaches were detached and the engine would return to Birmingham at the head of a parcels train.

Services to Manchester were also affected and for a period during the Summer of 1960 electrification work led to the temporary transfer of services away from London Road station. That had an interesting impact on the Monument Lane duties as the 7.10am and 12.10pm were diverted into Manchester Central and Manchester Victoria respectively. Bob Hardy recalled the workings and he believed that, together with driver Sid Cooper, he worked the first of the diversions into Manchester Central, when they handed over to a pilot driver from Northwich shed to take them into Central station. On that occasion they had a 'Royal Scot' 4-6-0, which gave the Northwich man a great deal of pleasure as he normally only worked on Stanier '8Fs'. Brian Clarke remembers that another pilot driver – and one who gave him a 'wet shirt' – was Jimmy Jones, one time Mayor of Northwich.

The 12.10pm worked via Stockport en route to Manchester Victoria. However, with that working a new locomotive and men took over from Stockport, whilst the Birmingham crew and engine retired to Edgeley shed, not a normal destination for workings from Monument Lane.

Once electrification work had been completed Monument Lane men came off at Crewe when on Manchester bound services and an electric locomotive took over. In the case of the 12.10pm, which by the end of 1960 was normally diesel hauled using an English Electric Type 4 (later Class 40), the men returned to New Street with the 3.30pm from Crewe, which originated in Glasgow. The train changed engines at Crewe, resulting at least once in the men experiencing 71000 *Duke of Gloucester* on the duty. Liverpool workings were not affected immediately and it was closure of the shed to steam that brought an end to those services.

The introduction of diesel multiple units led to the creation of a significant number of driving vacancies at the shed and an influx of men from a range of depots. Those men brought with them knowledge of a number of routes not usually familiar to men brought up on the Western Division lines and as a consequence there was at least one occasion when a special train over the Settle and Carlisle line had a Monument Lane man at the regulator. Dmus were also used on long journeys, reaching locations as diverse as Hull and Ramsgate.

Up to and including 1958 the Summer Saturday workings to Blackpool and Llandudno continued to make regular use of the shed's Compounds, with 40936 and 41168 making the journeys in 1958. Crewe North shed even borrowed 40936 in June of that year and it was reported piloting 'The Mid day Scot' from Carlisle to Crewe!

On Summer Saturdays in the late 1950s a Monument Lane 'Black 5' was employed on the 7.04am from Birmingham to Clacton. The locomotive, crewed by Rugby men, worked through to Ely before returning home with the 11.23am from Clacton to Birmingham. Steam was also used on 8 August 1959, when Class '5' 44807 worked a return special from Folkestone, which it took over in the London area. This special contained people returning from Lourdes.

In 1959 some of the Summer services to the coast did go over to DMU operation. On 8 August, for example, Metropolitan Cammell units including M50312/M50328 worked the 8.20am Smethwick to Llandudno train and M50315/M50333 and M50323/M50305 headed for the north west on the 9.15am from New Street to Morecambe. However, the City of Birmingham Holiday Express remained steam hauled into 1961, with 45071 including Blackpool amongst the destinations on 8 August of that year.

With closure to steam in February 1962 main line diesel locomotives continued to arrive at the former steam shed – primarily Class '24s' and Class '40s' – and the fitters would carry out superficial work, such as checking oil levels and topping up water. The men were instructed on both types, with Class '24' D5146 spending time in the area for crew training purposes.

Frank Ward's training took place between 2 and 13 April 1962 on a mix of Class '40s' and Class '24s'. Once his training had been completed, his first working was with the 6.25pm from New Street to Crewe – with 'Royal Scot' 46145! The next day he went even further back in time when he found himself on the footplate of one of the last surviving Johnson '2F' 0-6-0s in the West Midlands, taking 58124 light engine to Bescot.

As Monument Lane was solely a diesel multiple unit depot, the duties became increasingly local in nature. However, longer distance workings did not cease entirely, as the men continued to work to London, although trips beyond Crewe to the north west became increasingly rare.

When working the 10.40pm New Street to Euston parcels, the men returned the following afternoon, with an early evening working, such as the 5.22pm to Rugby via Northampton. The London workings included the 4.40pm Euston to Birmingham during the summer and the 4.30pm from Euston to Birmingham when the train was retimed for the winter. Another duty was the 5.15pm from Euston, normally with Class '40' or Class '24' locomotives.

However, Monument Lane men still found themselves on main line duties with steam. Such was the case on Friday 6 July 1962, when 45603 *Solomon Islands* worked from New Street to Stafford with the 8.59pm (FO) Coventry to Glasgow Central. On another occasion 'Jubilee' 45720 *Indomitable* hauled the 5.50pm from New Street to Liverpool as far as Crewe.

Soon came a form of steam power virtually unknown to men from the shed in earlier years when on Saturday 28 July 1962 there was no diesel available for the 4.40pm from Euston, and Camden had only 46246 *City of Manchester* available. The 4.40pm was a working on which steam appeared fairly frequently during the summer months of 1962. The 5.15pm ex Euston was another, usually with Class '5s', including the now preserved 45305 on 22 May 1962.

Steam was also evident when 70016 *Ariel* worked the 5.50pm to Crewe, whilst 'Black Five' 45333 provided the men with a rare chance to return to Manchester when it worked the 2.33pm from New Street on 8 June 1962. Then, on Monday May 20 1963, after working the 5.0pm from New Street to Euston with D305, the men returned on 46240 *City of Coventry* (1B) with a long standing Monument Lane turn, the 09.35pm from Euston to New St.

As the 1960s unfolded the 3.58pm to Rugby remained a Monument Lane duty, normally worked by Class '24s'. During 1965 Class '40s' appeared on the 15.58 duty, as they did on the 17.48 to Rugby. Class '40s' also gave the shed an out and back duty to London, with the 21.39 to Euston and 17.00 or 18.55 return.

By the mid 1960s work on the electrification of the ex LNW main line was well underway and that brought a great deal of piloting work when services were diverted away from the normal routes, such as the Stour Valley line. Such diversions took place, for example on Sunday 24 April and Sunday 1 May, resulting in assistance on Birmingham Snow Hill to Stafford workings via Bushbury.

Similarly the men acted as conductors during electrification of the Wolverhampton to Stafford section, which led to numerous diversions over the Princes End line. Amongst the last main line workings falling to the shed were the 17.25 from New Street to Rugby, and the 19.05 from Coventry to New Street, both of which used Class '40' power.

3

LOCAL AND SECONDARY PASSENGER SERVICES

The local lines around Birmingham and the West Midlands served by the LNWR, and later the LMS, provided a number of regular workings for Monument Lane men, although duties were shared with other sheds, such as Aston, Coventry, Bushbury, Walsall and Rugby. Lines worked regularly included:

- New Street to Lichfield City and Trent Valley via Sutton Coldfield;
- New Street to Rugby via Coventry and Leamington;
- New Street to Leamington (both via Coventry and via the Berkswell to Kenilworth line);
- New Street to Wolverhampton;
- New Street to Burton via Lichfield and Walsall;
- New Street to Stafford via Wolverhampton and via Rugeley;
- New Street to Stoke;
- Lichfield to Walsall via Brownhills.

On some of those services, Monument Lane men could also extend beyond the destinations listed, such as to Newcastle under Lyme and Silverdale in the Potteries and even to Tutbury prior to World War II. Workings beyond Leamington also reached Napton. Longer distance locals included Bletchley and Northampton and Shrewsbury via Stafford and Wellington. Occasionally, but more regularly with the arrival of DMUs, workings extended beyond Rugby to Peterborough.

THE LICHFIELD LINE

The principal local line worked was that to Lichfield, although some services terminated at Sutton Coldfield or Four Oaks.

Services on the Lichfield line altered markedly in 1955 when Monument Lane men were involved in the introduction of push-pull workings between New Street and Four Oaks. That move was no more than a temporary arrangement, however, as twelve months later, on 5 March 1956, the Lichfield line became the first in Birmingham to be converted to DMU operation. Thereafter, steam on the line's local workings became a rarity.

The line was the preserve, in the main, of larger tank locomotives. By the Edwardian era Whale's 4-4-2 tanks, such as 1985, frequently worked the trains and were noted by a contemporary traveller as 'completely masters of the job'. Bowen-Cooke 4-6-2 tanks ('Prince of Wales' Tanks) were also used, including 2665 (later 6950), which had a first class reputation. Also employed on the line were Webb's 0-6-2 'Watford Tanks' and 'Coal Tanks' would be requisitioned if there was a shortage of locomotives. One interesting feature before World War I was the use of a Crewe 'Precursor' or 'George V' on the 1.07pm (Saturdays only), which was borrowed after its arrival on a service from the north and was able to help out on a particularly demanding working which ran through to Erdington before stopping.

From the mid 1930s newly introduced taper boilered Class '4' tank locomotives took over, with the Fairburns 42262-65 and 42267 frequent performers during the late 1940s and early 1950s, usually well turned out for the prestigious businessmen's trains.

Although tank locomotives dominated, other classes played a part, too. Fowler '4F' 0-6-0s made regular appearances on certain trains, such as the 5pm from Monument Lane to Lichfield, and even as late as November 1948, 'Watford Tank' 58908 was to be found one evening at the head of the 5.40pm to Four Oaks, long after the class had ceased to be a regular choice for the line.

The shed's Compounds and 'Class 5s' would also be used on Lichfield trains and the 9.09am from Lichfield to New Street saw prestige power in the form of 'Royal Scot' 46151 on 18 October 1949. On two occasions LNW 0-8-0s were recorded as stand ins when Monument Lane locomotives failed, with 49278 and 49186 deputising on 14 October 1953 and 15 February 1955 respectively on the 8.20am from Sutton.

I also worked a Cauliflower to Lichfield on a morning trip when we were pushed for engines, tender first and not a very pleasant experience. (GD).

From April 1955, when services to Four Oaks went over to push-pull workings, three Ivatt Class '2' 2-6-2 tanks arrived at Monument Lane in the form of 41223, 41224 and 41320.

I was on the push pulls – men of my age were some of the youngest in the country on firing work. We had three little engines and two sets of coaches at the carriage shed. There was five weeks work on them and in that time we did seventy seven trips to Four Oaks without going anywhere else. (BC).

Following dieselisation services were worked initially by Derby Lightweight units before Metropolitan Cammell 3 car units (later Class 101) took over. They remained the mainstay up to, and after, Monument Lane's closure, although Brian Clarke also recalled the use of a Class '40' on the line on one occasion.

LOCALS BEYOND LICHFIELD

Monument Lane men were also responsible for working a number of services beyond Lichfield, including to Burton, Rugeley and Walsall via Brownhills.

One turn was the 7.50am passenger New Street to Burton via Lichfield. When we got to Burton the shunter detached us from our train as this was the usual practice on the Midland Railway. (FW).

On the 12.25pm New Street to Lichfield, when we got to Lichfield we were officially the shunt engine for the goods yard for a while, then we worked a train out of Lichfield via Walsall. I always remember what happened when we stopped at Brownhills station. Just as we were leaving, the Town Hall clock would strike five o'clock – day after day you would hear it. (BC).

As with the Lichfield line, services were normally worked with the larger tank engines.

The 7.50am to Burton was usually worked by a tank engine but on Wednesday 18 January 1956 we had 44506 as there was no tank engine available. (FW).

I once worked tender first to Rugeley with a 'Cauliflower'. We'd have our supper in the pub over the road. Then we worked a parcels over the Midland Road. With the 7.52am to Burton we went to Derby on Saturdays and came back to Coventry. (GD).

With the 7.37am to Rugeley we used to work a passenger down there, put the stock on one side and then work a trip up to the colliery at Brereton. Then we came back from Rugeley about dinner time. (BC).

BIRMINGHAM TO COVENTRY, RUGBY AND LEAMINGTON

Monument Lane men covered quite a mix of local services from New Street to Rugby and Leamington, some of which terminated at Coventry. Trains to Leamington had a choice of routes, proceeding either via Coventry and then Kenilworth or diverging at Berkswell onto the now closed line to Kenilworth. Trains using that route by-passed Coventry.

The occasional service to Leamington continued to Napton and Stockwell, on the line to Rugby. There was also an early morning working from Napton in the late 1930s, which, Jack Williams recalled, took a number of workers to the Woolworth's store in Leamington. In the 1950s the men worked an evening service to Napton, departing New Street at 5.08pm.

At one time, before the diagrams were altered, we used to have a Longsight Crab for the 5.08 to Leamington. They would then work back into New Street and get remanned for Longsight with a parcels train. Then we used to have a Warwick tankie on the job. We would book on in the afternoon, prepare the engine, go to the carriage shed, then down into New Street. We took the train to Berkswell, then went across the branch to Kenilworth, Warwick and Leamington, across the branch to Rugby and at Marton Junction we turned off and worked to Napton and Stockwell. Then we would run round the train and bring it back empty coaches to Leamington, put the engine on the shed at Warwick and then come back passenger to New Street. (BC).

The regular engine on this working in 1956 was Warwick's 42316, later replaced by 42566. In 1958 the passenger service to Napton was withdrawn.

Monument Lane duties to Rugby in the mid 1950s included the 2.50pm, 5.23pm and 6.26pm from New Street. The 6.26pm (later 6.30pm) reached Rugby via Marton Junction.

The majority of local workings fell to tank engines, although Class '5s' and the Compounds would make appearances and the '4Fs' were always on hand if needed. Unfortunately, on one occasion a Monument Lane working fell to an unexpected – and unwelcome – form of power.

One Saturday afternoon on a local to Leamington we had a Class '4F', 4514. She had a bad habit of the leading tender axle running hot and, true to form, this axle ran hot between Tile Hill and Canley, so we had to have another loco from Coventry and they did not have much to choose from. We finished up with a 'Super D' and we could not turn at Leamington. It was not a very pleasant trip, believe me. (CW).

There was a night time working to Leamington with the 2.50am parcels which returned in the morning at 7.55am via Kenilworth and Berkswell.

With the 7.55 the Berkswell branch had a hell of a bank and often we would get stuck, so they eventually gave us an assistant engine. That was a Class '2' passenger engine, 508, which was reallocated from Aston and she was the regular pilot engine. (RL).

We used to book on just after 1 o'clock in the morning with a big 'Scot' more likely than not, with 11 on and go down into New Street to work the 2.50 to Leamington. On arrival we'd back them into the siding, go up to Warwick to fill the tank, turn it, back down onto the stock and stand on it – in the winter we would steam heat it. Then in the morning we used to stop at Warwick, Kenilworth, then across the branch to Berkswell, cutting out Coventry, then Berkswell, Hampton in Arden, Marston Green, Stechford, where we filled the tank, and into New Street, where we were relieved for Liverpool. (BC).

For a time the working was diagrammed for a Crewe North locomotive and they would often take the opportunity to use a locomotive released from Crewe Works for running-in turns.

There was also a regular working for a Monument Lane engine, usually a Compound or Fairburn tank, in the 1950s but which had Coventry men on the footplate. The service began as the 4.35pm from Leamington to Wolverhampton, after which the engine returned light to New Street, still with the Coventry crew. After a break, the crew took the engine light engine to New Street to work the 10.55pm all stations to Coventry.

LOCALS BEYOND RUGBY

During the immediate post war period the shed worked local services beyond Rugby. The destinations included Bletchley and Northampton at different times. The Northampton service returned with the 12.23pm Northampton to New Street. This could be a most interesting working on Saturdays as it often boasted two locomotives for part of the journey, including, at times, two Compounds; eventually the 8.45am ran to Peterborough. For a period, Monument Lane men also would work locals from Euston to Bletchley before returning on another local to Birmingham via Northampton.

BIRMINGHAM TO WALSALL AND WOLVERHAMPTON

Men and engines worked some local services to Wolverhampton and Walsall, usually with Class '4' tanks.

Walsall workings could also be part of turns to Brownhills and the locomotive required for one of the Saturday morning holiday trips first worked a local to Walsall and then returned from Brownhills before changing crews at New Street.

STAFFORD, THE POTTERIES AND SHREWSBURY

Some services extended to Stafford and the Potteries, such as two services which left at 5.55am, one to Stafford and one to Stoke, albeit taking different routes, via Wolverhampton and via Rugeley.

The 5.55 to Stafford was a big engine, we used to work all stations via Walsall, Cannock and Rugeley to Stafford, where we got remanned by a Stafford man. We then walked across the platform and we relieved a Stoke man – we always knew it as the Silverdale – with an Aston tankie. We used to work back into New Street, take the empty stock to Vauxhall and then the engine onto Aston shed, dispose of it and get the bus back to Monument Lane. (BC).

We had a regular Stoke on Trent job – 5.55am. It was a local, all stations to Stafford, on to the shed and turn the engine, a big tankie and then work bunker first to Stoke and then down to Newcastle under Lyme, return to Stoke, back on to some coaches in the carriage sidings and then work to New Street, take the empty stock out to Vauxhall and return light engine to the shed. The regular engine on that job was 42674, an outstanding engine. (BC).

The train was the 5.55am and 8.30am Stoke to Newcastle under Lyme. When the diesels arrived we worked through to Silverdale. (CW).

THE HARBORNE LINE

One other route that fell within the network of local passenger trains worked by Monument Lane men and engines was the Harborne line which closed in 1934. Passenger duties were shared with Walsall but on the last day of operation 6924 and 7742 – both Monument Lane engines – worked the line. At one time, top link men would work to Harborne before returning and continuing to London on a separate main line train.

SPECIALS

Special trains have been operated for sporting events for many years. One earlier example was a special to Sutton Coldfield races in 1884, which comprised ten first class coaches. Post war a regular working involved taking over specials – usually football specials – from the ex GW lines.

We worked football specials, usually to Villa Park, which originated from the Western. The Western would bring them in from Stourbridge and Kidderminster. We'd take them over at Galton Junction and work them round the city through Soho Road and stop at Aston station, put them into Vauxhall sidings and stay with them until the match was over, then take them back the same way. A spur road ran down the side of the main line and their engine would wait there. (GD).

I remember going up to Galton Junction light engine. A Stourbridge train came in with a Western Region pannier tank on. He hooked off and we took the train to Sutton Coldfield – it was a Sunday school outing. When we hooked on we had to pull the chord to equal the vacuum. The Western Region blew 25" of vacuum and we only blew 21", so we had to pull the chords to even the brakes up. (BC).

The duties were normally entrusted to the one of the depot's tank locomotives, although on 10 September 1949 Compound 1111 set off tender first from Galton Junction for Witton station. The football specials used the short spur at Soho Soap Works Junction to gain access to the Soho Road line. In doing so they used a short section of track which did not have a regular passenger service.

One of the more unusual workings occurred on 14 July 1951, when 44057 reached Northamptonshire on a railtour. Certainly 3E locomotives worked to that county almost on a daily basis but never via the Stratford & Midland Joint Railway as 44057 did that day, working the train throughout from New Street.

Steam power had also worked a Stephenson Locomotive Society Special on 30 May 1959. The veteran 0-6-0 58271 circled Birmingham over several hours, covering the Harborne line and such out of the way spots (for a Monument Lane engine) as the Longbridge to Halesowen branch.

Once diesel multiple units had arrived they covered an increasing number of lines, including those to Coventry, Wolverhampton and Leamington. They were also pressed into service on longer runs and the 8.45am to Peterborough was an early convert and before long they were employed on Sunday excursions, such as to Oxford and Trentham Gardens. Nevertheless, some services to Rugby retained steam workings well into the DMU era. The 5.48pm from New Street to Rugby, for example, was rostered for steam haulage in 1961.

Most unusually, on August 11th 1964 a working from Birmingham New Street reached the former Great Western Railway's Low Level station. The train, an Officers' Special, was conducted by Frank Ward and travelled via Bescot and

Heath Town Junction. The locomotive involved was BR Standard Tank 80072, which is now preserved.

Overall, the arrival of DMUs brought about a pattern of working that would remain relatively unchanged throughout the early 1960s, comprising local services on ex LNW routes around Birmingham, including those to Lichfield, Walsall, Wolverhampton, Coventry and Rugeley, interspersed with longer trips to Stafford, Stoke and Northampton and now Peterborough. In 1966 the men also began to take in new routes on the former Great Western lines from Birmingham Snow Hill to Wolverhampton Low Level, Kidderminster and Leamington Spa and from Dudley to Stourbridge.

By the mid 1960s some services were being withdrawn and Frank Ward worked the last passenger train from Nuneaton to Leamington Spa Avenue on Saturday 16 January 1965. It was also the last train to call at Warwick Milverton and Kenilworth.

Finally, in 1967 the men began to train on the new electric multiple units, working them on local services such as to Walsall and Wolverhampton before the shed closed in March 1967.

4

GOODS AND SHUNTING DUTIES

During the early years of the shed's life the men would work a mix of local and longer distance freight services. Eventually, most of Monument Lane's responsibilities for goods work involved local workings or trip and shunting duties for goods yards within just a few miles of the shed. To the end the men might find themselves booked to Crewe or Rugby on a special freight duty, but in later years they were normally confined to Wolverhampton, Bescot and the extremities of the Harborne branch.

GOODS YARDS & BRANCHES

Stour Valley

In 1883 the goods yards on the Stour Valley line were covered by two locomotive turns – known as Stour Valley 1 and Stour Valley 2. Monument Lane covered Stour Valley 2 and Bushbury took responsibility for Stour Valley 1. In 1883, the Monument Lane locomotive was on duty from 6.10am to 6.55pm Monday to Saturday, covering Soho, Smethwick Junction, Spon Lane, Spon Lane Basin, Dudley Port, Albion and Oldbury.

There were separate arrangements for the Harborne branch and at that time Tipton was the responsibility of Bushbury; ultimately it fell to Monument Lane. Then, as traffic built up, there was a requirement for the use of additional locomotives, with a number of the yards justifying their own engines.

We worked Monument Lane yard, Soho Pool, the Harborne branch, Soho New Sidings (known as Soho Tip, now the site of the Diesel and Electric Depot), Soho Yard, where, on the right, there was a branch into Averys, then a branch for the coal and gas into Smethwick Gas Works. Then you got Oldbury yard – quite a big busy yard, where a lot of heavy shunting went on. After that you came to Albion with its residential engine. The yard at Spon Lane had a shed where they loaded some of Chance's glass, and then through Spon Lane station the next yard was Spon Lane Basin, as it says, built on the side of the canal. The next one was Dudley Port, followed by Tipton, with a yard either side of the main line and another residential engine. Monument Lane men only worked to Tipton, others were covered by Bushbury. (BC).

Malthouse Sidings

Malthouse Sidings were situated directly opposite the locomotive depot. Originally linked to a brewery – hence its name – the sidings also served a coal yard and were used to stable wagons bringing coal to the depot.

Monument Lane Goods Depot

Monument Lane was the largest of the yards shunted by the shed's engines. Situated just a stone's throw from the engine shed, Monument Lane Goods Yard ran alongside the down main line. Many of the services ran to local destinations such as Wolverhampton and Bescot, where they would be formed into longer distance services. However, a small number of express freights worked directly to more distant locations including Manchester, Leeds and Mold Junction in North Wales. There were also local workings to Shrewsbury and Wichnor Junction, between Lichfield and Burton on Trent, carrying exchange traffic for Derby and the North.

For many years the yard was covered by a three shift duty, with only a brief respite between 10pm and 1am, Mondays to Saturdays. The site included a large goods shed, known for many years as the 'Bedstead Shed', as a local factory used it as the distribution point for its products, some of which were destined for overseas Heads of State. Coal played an important part, too, mainly originating from the South Staffordshire collieries around Norton Junction and Angelsea on the Walsall to Lichfield line.

Monument Lane men were mainly responsible for shunting the yard, with Bushbury, Bescot and Aston men working many of the freight trains elsewhere. The goods yard was normally worked by tender locomotives, such as 'Cauliflowers' and 'Coal Engines'. The Johnson '2F' 0-6-0s then became the normal choices, with 58273 a regular performer, followed by 58124 and examples such as 58220 still representing the class in the late 1950s.

Soho

The first yard on the down line was Soho New Sidings, always known as Soho Tip. The Soho Tip engine was only one shift, which we brought back at dinner time. The loco would shunt Soho Tip as required and would also go up and shunt Smethwick as required, such as taking the loads up and bringing the empties back. Perhaps there would be some coaches they wanted putting together to make excursions for the weekend.

On the other side was Soho yard itself, which had its own shunt engine. That would shunt from around 2 o'clock in the morning to around midnight, then go back to the shed. (BC).

Smethwick

At Smethwick station there were very small sidings either side of the main line. There was a coal wharf on the up side and on the down side was a goods shed – a lot of potatoes went in there to Sam Price's. (BC).

Albion

The goods yard at Albion serviced a number of factories, many related to metalworking. At one time the locomotive also worked a train to Bescot. There was also an evening working to Exchange Sidings.

For one evening train, we'd book on and get an engine ready then take it to Lichfield and back. Then we'd leave the coaches in New Street, take the engine on shed, have our supper and then we'd do light engine to Albion sidings for a freight. At the time that was the only freight to work through the tunnel into New Street. We took it to Exchange Sidings a mile or so from New Street from where it went on to Avonmouth and Bristol. (GD).

That particular working was timetabled away from Albion at 11.30pm, with the locomotive returning to the shed from Exchange Sidings. Later the working originated from Tipton, picking up at Albion, Oldbury and sometimes Dudley Port.

Spon Lane

The sidings at Spon Lane were a two shift job and the timetables identified two separate sites, Spon Lane and Spon Lane Basin, alongside the Birmingham to Wolverhampton Canal. Spon Lane was also the site of Chance Bros Glass Works, which generated a significant amount of rail traffic.

The Basin was a piece of cake. The rails had been down for about a hundred years and could only take a little engine – a little 'Gadget' (Coal Tank) or something like that. You had a shunter there and the engine would come over with a trip. It was a down side shunt and they would put it off at the Basin. Then the engine would come over from Oldbury. In 1955 it was mostly pig iron and women used to unload it. (RL)

In the 1940s, 3231, a Midland '3F', was the regular Spon Lane engine. Midland '2Fs' also worked the yard and it provided work for the shed's last 'Cauliflower', 58427.

The first firing job I had was Saturday afternoon at 2 o'clock. I went to Spon Lane and when we got there it was an old 'Cauliflower'. It was all glass from Chance's Glass Works but everything was done at a sedate pace and they even used horses. (LR).

Oldbury

As with Spon Lane, Oldbury was a two shift job.

There were sixteen roads in Oldbury yard and they used to unload big stuff onto the wagons. They went to all of the steelworks at Tipton and Oldbury. (RL).

After the Oldbury engine went back to the shed, the late night Spon Lane engine went across and shunted Oldbury. When they'd shunted at Oldbury they came down to Soho, finished the shunting there and then it was back to the shed by around 2 o'clock in the morning. Oldbury, Monument Lane and Soho were almost 24 hour shifts. (BC).

After the era of the 'Cauliflowers' and 'Coal Engines', Midland and LMS '4Fs' worked at Oldbury and 3915 and later 44057 were the regular engines because they were right hand drive, allowing easier visibility based on the way that the yard was laid out.

Tipton

The engine at Tipton shunted the local goods yard and also worked to Bloomfield twice a day. There was also a mid day trip to Mond Gas Sidings to take coke and bring back empties.

When we came off the shed at 5 o'clock we used to go to Bloomfield. There were wagons at Bloomfield and there was a horse driver and chain lad who did the shunting when we weren't there. At Bloomfield there was a big canal basin and we used to have to get about 60 wagons into position. There was a lot of pig iron there as well as long iron steel billets. I've been to the rolling mills at Bloomfield and some of it had to be hand lifted until they put a crane in.

When I first went to Tipton there were furnaces at Tipton and we used to bring in a train load of coke from Bloomfield to Tipton and take it up to the furnace sidings. We had to go so far down the line and have a run to get up the bank.

We used to shunt Mond Gas Sidings in the afternoon, going from Tipton with a little train. Then we used to have to get the empties out and take them to Dudley Port and put them in the sidings there for the night train to Tipton. Back to Tipton and it would be about five o'clock when we had some vans that they used to load with sausage. We used to get them out of the dock and put them on a train at about half past five and we used to have another one at half past nine. When we put the one on at half past nine we used to go to Bloomfield and shunt at night. We had no waiting time. (GC).

By the 1950s there were similar duties to undertake.

We shunted the yards at Tipton and Bloomfield, Dudley Port, the goods shed at Tipton and Tipton Gas Works. We would get different jobs at different times of the year. We had one job attaching a sausage van from Palethorpe's yard onto the Stoke train at 4 o'clock in the afternoon. The goods were mainly steel, including girders, billets and pig iron. Also included were parts for street lights made by Revo. We took the sludge from local sheds to be emptied close to Tipton, carried in old loco tenders. In later years we went over to Wednesbury to bank engines through to Princes End. (AP).

The sludge from local sheds was transported to the nearby siding of the Tipton Sewage Disposal Works, where there was a sludge disposal plant.

Soho Pool

Monument Lane men were also involved in shunting at Soho Pool. Soho Pool was at the end of a short branch off the Perry Barr to Soho loop, which opened in 1887. It was a busy location, including a Regent petroleum depot, Trinidad Limmer asphalt plant, a timber yard and numerous coal sidings. The branch was situated on a heavily graded line, so Monument Lane men also undertook banking duties for outward workings.

At one end of Soho triangle was Soho East box. They had a woman when I first went there – we used to take a churn of water. The Pool engine did it every morning as they used to shut it at night. Soho Road station was there but it was shut. You ran past the station and then crossed over and we had to pick up the staff because it was single line down into the Pool. Trains were coming in and out of there from Bescot all day long and we used to have to bank them out. We had a morning turn and afternoon turn and on the afternoon turn we used to have to work a train to Bescot on our own. There was a train came in first – usually a 'D' from Bescot – and he used to bank us out and we used go to Bescot and have about an hour there, and then work back into

Monument Lane. Coming round from Perry Barr up to Handsworth Wood there was a little siding with a water softening plant. Aston men had a 2F there permanently for pushing trains up the bank. When I first went to Soho Pool our engines were 22920 and 22928. (GD).

On the afternoon trip the signalman would ring down to the cabin and say that the banker was here. We used to go up to Soho Road, hook onto the Aston bank engine, take it down to the Pool and it would get behind our train and bank us out – we could have around 45 loose coupled wagons on with that train. 44592 was the star engine on that working because she had a dry steam brake, an independent steam brake that could be worked without having the vacuum brake on. (BC).

Stechford

Although the shed did not send a shunting engine to Stechford, it did have some freight work to the yard. One duty involved a light engine movement to Four Oaks, after which the locomotive worked a passenger train to New Street. It then proceeded light engine to Adderley Park, where it picked up a freight train and worked it to Stechford. From Stechford it moved on to Monument Lane, dropping off wagons at Witton and Soho Road.

THE HARBORNE BRANCH

Close to the depot was the Harborne branch, which left the Birmingham to Wolverhampton Stour Valley route between Monument Lane and Winson Green stations. Although it lost its passenger services back in 1934, the branch remained open to freight until 1963.

This was a fairly busy freight duty, with a coal yard at Hagley Road, brewery traffic for the Mitchells and Butlers' sidings at Cape Hill and a mixture of goods at Harborne. Some of the trains were well loaded, for example in 1905 the 5.15am from Monument Lane could set out with fifteen trucks and pick up a further twenty at Hagley Road, all of which were loaded.

We'd do about five trips each day up the branch. In the 1940s the first trip of the morning was the 5.10am to Mitchells and Butlers and then we'd do another trip before breakfast, right through to Harborne, where there was a Chad Valley factory. The third train of the day involved shunting Hagley Road.

Just after joining the branch was Summerfield Park and my mate had an allotment there, including a hut with an old pot bellied stove. The drivers would kick big lumps of coal off the engine for him. (GD).

Whilst in the 1950s, when Brian Clarke was on the footplate.

We used to take a lot of coal for the coal wharf at Hagley Road and Harborne itself. That was the main traffic there in my day. Sometimes we would fetch sand out of Harborne. It was quite a sharp climb up to Hagley Road so you just plodded up and then you would drop down to Rotton Park and Icknield Port Road. You used to work them flat out if you had about sixteen loads of coal, full regulator to get up the line. (BC).

It was a very hot summer and we had quite a load on with a Midland '2'. We were going towards Rotton Park and I threw the engine right over onto second regulator. Sparks were flying everywhere and when I came back there were five fire engines fighting the fires. (RN).

We worked to Mitchells and Butlers' sidings to take the malt and then we came back light engine. We used to have a staff to get into the brewery sidings then brewery men would come to get them with their engine.

Then we went 9.10 to Mitchells with the same engine and brake van and we'd take the coal, putting off at Hagley Road. Then we'd shunt Harborne and come back with just engine and brake. Then we'd take the loco coal out of Malthouse Sidings onto the loco, and then take out the empties to Monument Lane goods. The engine went off again at 3.10pm to Mitchells and we also went to Harborne, where we shunted and picked up around twenty empty vans back to Hagley Road and shunt Hagley Road. We had red moulding sand and they would send a man up from Monument Lane at night to sheet it down. We got back on the shed about 9.30pm – it was two shifts. (RL).

Although the depot had responsibility for working goods trains serving the brewery, the sidings themselves were in the hands of M&B's own two locomotives.

Mitchells and Butlers had their own locos but we used to hire out engines if they had problems and I remember a couple of Lancashire and Yorkshire 'Pugs' being used for the job, including the preserved 51218. We used to go into their sidings just past the old Rotton Park station, where we'd drop coal and wagons with empty barrels and crates. Their engine would come down the sidings to meet us near the BR line. Whenever we shunted their yard at Cape Hill they used to give us a chit to buy a pint from the brewery. (GD).

When we brought the beer from Mitchells and Butlers in very hot weather there was a block of ice on top of each barrel. We also used to bring Guinness down to a warehouse at Monument Lane and if you did that shunt for them you were given a Guinness. (RN).

Goods duties on the branch were shared amongst a number of classes, including Webb Tanks, Johnson '2F' 0-6-0s and 'Cauliflowers'.

FACTORY SIDINGS

There were also factory sidings to work on the Stour Valley line.

In the 1940s there was a regular working to Avery's. They had around 40 wagons of coal every day. We used to push them over and their Peckett would take over. It would also push out the empties and we'd put them into the sidings at Soho Tip on the opposite side of the line. (GD).

Avery's was on the angle on the up line when you came to Soho Soap Works. You would turn for the Soho Road line and there was a branch into the factory at that point The Soho Tip engine would take the Avery's traffic down during the day and would also shunt Smethwick.

On the loop between Soho Tip and Soho yard on the down side of the line was Wiggins factory. There was a very steep climb out on that line and you had to be careful with the level of water in the boiler.

We had another job that we called 'The Sausage'. We used to go light engine from Monument Lane to Dudley Port. We'd then go round the corner to Sedgley Junction, shunt the vans and fetch the loaded vans of sausage out of Palethorpe's factory, bringing them back up the main line, then we used to work them down to Stafford. At one time we used to go light engine in front of the express, the 2.00pm to Liverpool. After a while they decided that rather than send this engine light, we would drop down into the station and give them a pull as far as Dudley Port. We hooked off there, went off the main line and stood on the canal bridge. Sometimes we would actually take van loads of pigs down to the factory. (BC).

One other feature of a trip to Palethorpes was that the crew could watch the company groundsman Jack Holden running around his grounds. He was a former marathon runner who took part in the 1948 Olympic Games in London.

OTHER GOODS DUTIES

In the early years of the shed freight trains regularly worked through New Street station. That necessity was removed with the opening of the Soho to Perry Barr line on 1 March 1888 which gave access from all of the goods yards on the Stour Valley to the southern side of Birmingham, where Stechford developed as an interchange point.

At one time the depot also worked to Shrewsbury on what was known as the 'Salop Goods'. That working, though, disappeared by the early 1940s. There was also an evening coke working from Windsor Street sidings, which left the main line virtually opposite Aston depot.

There were one or two other regular freight workings and other occasional work.

At 3.25 in the morning we'd go down the bank to Bescot, then go across to Pleck and go onto Bushbury shed and then work back along the Stour. (GD).

One other 'goods' duty is worthy of mention.

We had another job from September onwards when we would take coal to the signalboxes. On Sundays we would set out with about three coal wagons and some labourers, stopping at all of the boxes and even some stations. (GD).

LONG DISTANCE WORKINGS

William Woods, who worked at the shed from 1879 to 1928, recalled piloting express goods trains to Liverpool and Manchester in the 1890s.

Although those duties reduced over the years, longer distance work could still arise to the locations such as Crewe and London, albeit usually on special trains.

The Specials could take many forms. One such example was the 'Scenery Specials', which moved the equipment for different shows that were touring the country. One ran on Easter Sunday 1953, loading at Central Goods before being worked into New Street. Monument Lane men then took it on to Willesden with a 'Black 5', providing Brian Clarke with his first trip to London.

THE DIESEL ERA

Freight duties continued to be relatively unchanged in the late 1950s, although there was increasing evidence of a movement to road transport. One duty of the early 1960s was an out and back trip to Bushbury, leaving Monument Lane in the evening. This was a '4F' duty which, in traditional style, called at a number of yards on its journey to drop off or pick up wagons. On another working the men took a freight from Willesden to Bescot, using a Stanier '8F'.

In 1963 the local goods network began to shrink, when in November the Harborne branch closed. Ironically, steam returned briefly on 12 and 13 February when two Class '2' Ivatt 2-6-0s, 46421 and 46456 were summoned in the place of the usual Class '03', no doubt caused by the continuing freezing weather conditions during a very bad winter.

Ballast' workings were also an aspect of the work undertaken by Monument Lane men, often with Stanier '8Fs', and on 25 August 1963 Frank Ward was at New Street with the steam crane on the footplate of 70000 *Britannia*.

The goods yards would be visited by main line diesels. However, one such visit was of a type not usually seen when on Friday 19 March 1965, Frank Ward conducted Western Region men with a Soho Pool to Dudley tanker train hauled by a Hymek diesel!

There was one other increasingly frequent activity in the goods yards – the need to send for the breakdown train from the shed to rerail wagons. The sidings at M&B and Albion were particularly prone to problems in their final years.

Monument Lane men also took an Ivatt Class '2' off the shed to work a demolition train on the remains of the Hampton in Arden to Whitacre line. There is a view that this may have been the last steam locomotive to leave the shed, around 1964. The train was worked back to Curzon Street and the locomotive returned light engine to Aston.

PARCELS SERVICES

The shed was involved in the operation of a number of parcels and newspaper trains, including the 12.05am from Crewe to New Street, the 2.50am from New Street to Leamington, the 3.19am from Rugby to New Street and the 10.40pm from New Street right through to London.

We booked on at 11.25 at night to work the 12.05 parcels from Crewe, which was 24 vans to New Street (RL).

North from New Street on the main line was a night turn for men in 1A link, the 12.02 parcels to Stafford.

We always left New Street out of the coffee bay which was next to Platform 6. On arrival at Stafford we had about three hours there and worked the Leeds parcels back. (FW).

We had the 2.50am Leamington mail, which was a Crewe engine, usually a 'Jubilee' or a 'Scot' but sometimes a 'Black 5'. We worked to Coventry then to Leamington. We'd put the coaches in the sidings and take the engine onto the shed, do the fire and get her ready. Incidentally, the Leamington mail even ran on Christmas morning. (GD).

There was also the 10.40pm from New Street.

From Wolverhampton the engine used to work a local into New Street, hook off and back up onto the shed. We would reman it, go back into New Street into No 1 bay at the south end of the station and we would stand on one van, which would then be loaded with registered mail. Most of the train would then be brought into New Street from Central Goods by a Saltley man. He would hook off and we would come out of the bay with the one van. Then we would back up on to the train and away we would go with anything up to 20 vans.

At Coventry we picked up again and then we used to go to Bletchley where we lost a lot of the train. We would keep one van then work into Euston. We would take the engine up to Camden then we would ride with a Bushbury man who was going light engine to Watford and he would drop us off at Willesden, where we would go into the loco and book off.

Later the working was altered, and instead of putting off at Bletchley we used to put off at Blisworth. We used to go inside and remarshall the train then we would go inside at Kilburn where there was a temporary parcels depot while they were rebuilding Euston, but we would still retain the one van of registered mail which we would work into Euston. (BC).

Another local working was the 5.15am to Wolverhampton, which was rostered for a Bushbury '6P' locomotive in the mid 1950s.

At Christmas Monument Lane Goods shed was taken over to help deal with the additional mail traffic for the Birmingham area.

A fortnight before Christmas, Monument Lane goods shed was taken over by the GPO and used as a sorting office. Then we'd work them up to Maiden Lane with a Compound. I remember going up one night and we picked up a pilot – I think that it was a Watford Midland '2P' – from Rugby. We shut off after Bushey troughs but he couldn't shut the regulator – there were sparks flying everywhere. (GD).

At Christmas we used to borrow a Super 'D' from Bescot to work the post office mails up and down from New Street to Monument Lane. (BC).

I fired on the last Christmas Day parcels train of 1959 from Monument Lane to Derby on 42951 (Crewe South). Arthur Venables was my driver. We were relieved at Derby and asked to work a freight train back to Washwood Heath, then take the engine to Saltley. (FW).

We booked on towards Christmas on a Thursday at 8.20pm. We were taking a special parcels train to Crewe. It was about 10.20 when we left the yard and it was getting pretty foggy. By the time you got to Wolverhampton you couldn't see your hand in front of you. In fact I was climbing signal posts to see if the signals were on or off. We didn't get to Crewe until about 9 o'clock the next morning. (BS).

Monument Lane men also took over a newspaper train at New Street after it had worked through from London.

Although Monument Lane did not play a major role in operating the fastest trains between Birmingham and London, its locomotives did head the two hour expresses from time to time. One of the shed's new Compounds, 1178, is at New Street station in September 1926 waiting to take over one of the London 2 hour expresses. *LNWR Society Collection/LNWRS 2360.*

The first Stanier Class '5' to arrive at Monument Lane in the 1930s was 5131 during week ending 7 March 1936. It is heading the 10.10am from Birmingham to Euston shortly afterwards on 24 May 1936. *LCGB/Ken Nunn collection.*

All of the depot's Class '5's left in 1941 and no examples returned until 1946. That meant that the shed had to rely on its Compound 4-4-0s when using its own engines on its principal expresses. 1116 has worked to London and is turning at Camden shed on 9 June 1945. *H C Casserley*.

In June 1953 two hour expresses were reintroduced between Birmingham and London and Monument Lane locomotives were called on the assist some of workings. That duty frequently fell to Compounds and 41090 is all set to pilot Bushbury 'Jubilee' 45592 *Indore* to London in the early days of the accelerated service, on Monday 19 June 1953, with the 4.05pm from Wolverhampton High Level to Euston. As the new service settled down it became more usual for Monument Lane to assist only the heavier trains on Fridays and Saturdays. The Compound will have joined the train at Birmingham. *Ben Stone*.

Compound 40933 has now acquired 40936's high sided tender. It is at Clifton Road, Rugby, piloting Bushbury's 45703 *Thunderer* with the 11.55am Wolverhampton to Euston on 9 April 1954. *Roger Shenton.*

On 3 August 1957 Compound 40936 pilots Bushbury 'Jubilee' 45709 *Implacable* past Carpenders Park. The service is thought to be the Saturday counterpart for the down 'Midlander'. *C R L Coles/Rail Archive Stephenson.*

Wherever possible the shed would use 'Class 5s' instead of Compounds, and the days of the 4-4-0 on these workings were almost over on 28 June 1957 as 3E's 45034 assists on the down 'Midlander'. *LCGB/Ken Nunn collection.*

Heavy snow fall and freezing temperatures overnight in the northern part of the country have left their mark as Monument Lane Class '5' 45071 waits to assist 'Britannia' 70033 *Charles Dickens* at New Street on the 7.50am from Wolverhampton to New Street on 25 February 1958. It is almost 9.15, so the train is already around 45 minutes late. *Michael Mensing.*

Caprotti valve 'Black 5' 44742 is waiting to leave Manchester (London Road) with the 4.30pm to Birmingham on 9 April 1960. This was the return working of the 12.20pm Birmingham to Manchester, a long standing Monument Lane working albeit with a 'foreign' locomotive since 1956. The driver standing on the platform is Sid Cooper. *Michael Mensing*.

Rebuilt 'Royal Scot' 46120 *Royal Inniskilling Fusilier* is leaving Crewe with the Liverpool portion of the 9.15am from New Street on 27 September 1960. The train also conveyed a portion for Manchester, which has now separated from the train and electric traction will take it forward. *Michael Mensing*.

The shed had a collection of tank locomotives of various sizes to work its local passenger services. One of the smaller examples, Class '1P' 2-4-2 1393, is at New Street in June 1927. *L W Perkins/F A Wycherley Collection.*

The much larger Superheater 4-6-2 tank 2670 is standing in Platform 2 at Birmingham New Street with a Four Oaks to New Street local train in June 1926. *LNWR Society Collection/ LNWRS 2372.*

'Prince of Wales' Tank 6950 at New Street on 9 February 1936. Monument Lane had a small allocation of these powerful locomotives for many years. The final three, including 6950, left for Bangor in July of the same year. *L W Perkins/F A Wycherley Collection.*

It would not be possible to illustrate one of Monument Lane's local workings without including one of the 'Watford Tanks', such as 6876, which did yeoman service for many years around the Birmingham area. *L Hanson.*

Monument Lane sent out a mixture of locomotives on the last day of passenger services on the Harborne branch on 24 November 1934, including 'Watford Tanks', 'Coal Tanks' and 2-4-2 tanks, such as 6755, shown at Harborne. *L W Perkins/F A Wycherley Collection.*

A number of new Fairburn tank engines came to the shed in the late 1940s, including 42267, seen here at New Street on 29 July 1961 with the 1.12pm from Ely. This service was actually booked for a DMU by this date and 42267 will have taken over at Rugby. *D Forsyth/ P Chancellor Collection.*

Fowler Class '4' tank 42421 is taking water at Lichfield Trent Valley High Level Station on the 10.32am Burton to New Street on 5 February 1955. The engine will have reached Burton on the 7.50am from New Street. The water point at Lichfield was a difficult one to operate and the firemen has enlisted some help to work it. *Roger Shenton.*

As was the case at many sheds, Monument Lane would call on its '4Fs' to work passenger trains at times and they had regular workings on the Lichfield line in the 1940s and 1950s. 44512 has a relatively light train on just such a duty. *John Hicks.*

Ivatt Tank 41224 stands at Sutton Coldfield station in July 1955 on one of the push pull workings introduced to Sutton and Four Oaks as a prelude to the DMU services from March 1956. *T J Edgington.*

An extremely grimy Compound 1153 stands at Watford on 26 July 1947 with a parcels working. Despite its external appearance the Compound appears steam tight, which is as it should be as the locomotive underwent a heavy general repair barely four months earlier. This was around the beginning of a period when the shed had great difficulty in recruiting cleaners, a situation that would never improve significantly. *H C Casserley.*

'Cauliflower' 0-6-0 28616 is shunting at Harborne in July 1949. The yard produced a mixture of goods, including coal and moulding sand. Later renumbered 58427, the locomotive remained at Monument Lane until week ending 8 April 1950, making it the last 'Cauliflower' to work at the shed. *M Whitehouse Collection/courtesy R Carpenter.*

'Watford Tank' 6894 is on the branch freight climbing away from Harborne around May 1947. The locomotive was withdrawn during week ending 24 May 1947, which means that this is one of its last duties. *M Whitehouse Collection/courtesy R Carpenter.*

58178 is in Malthouse Sidings, so named because Mitchell's brewery (one half of Mitchells and Butlers) was located to the rear of the train. Monument Lane shed is directly opposite Malthouse Sidings, which were used to stable coal destined for the shed, and 58178 is no doubt about to transfer a new consignment across to the depot. This particular duty was usually carried out by the engine working the Harborne branch. *D J Norton.*

Coal Tank 46912 passes Mond Gas Sidings Signal Box on 24 August 1950 with what seems to be a train of empty wagons. This particular duty fell to the locomotive outstationed at Tipton shed and usually took place around mid day. *M Whitehouse Collection/courtesy R Carpenter.*

Work stained '4F' 44444 is leaving the sidings near the site of Soho station on the evening of 8 June 1961 on a down freight. This was the only locomotive on the BR network to have the same five numerals and is probably working the shed's evening duty to Bushbury, which called at a number of yards en route. *Michael Mensing.*

Monument Lane had responsibility for station pilot duties on the Western lines side of New Street. Those duties required the services of two engines, one at each end of the station, and usually employed engines past the first flush of youth. 'Special Tank' 3615 is on South End Shunt duties in May 1925. The locomotive is coupled to an LNWR elliptical roof full brake in LNWR livery. *LNWR Society Collection/LNWRS 2362.*

A more unusual south end shunt locomotive on 23 April 1935 is LMS '3F' 0-6-0T 7231. *L W Perkins/F A Wycherley Collection.*

Locomotives on north end station pilot duties at New Street were passenger locomotives as they might be called on to assist trains in trouble through to Dudley Port or Wolverhampton. Veteran 'Watford Tank' 46900 is undertaking some shunting at the north end on 14 August 1951. *M Whitehouse Collection/courtesy R Carpenter.*

A virtually brand new Class '2' 2-6-2T 41214 is acting as the New Street south end pilot on 25 September 1948. After years of having to use Victorian and Edwardian locomotives this must have been the height of luxury to the Monument Lane men, but it was to be a short lived experiment. Within a few weeks the locomotive was transferred to Plodder Lane and it was back to the old days, as the Coal Tanks returned to New Street! *D J Norton*.

In the early 1950s Jubilee 45601 *British Guiana* has arrived at the shed for servicing after working one the British Industries Fair specials. Camden men worked the trains to Birmingham and Monument Lane covered the return journey. *Howard Turvey*.

For a time in 1950 ex Lancashire and Yorkshire Railway 'Pug' 51218 came to Monument Lane. The locomotive was then loaned to Mitchells and Butlers to work their sidings at Cape Hill, as the company's own locomotives were out of action. The 'Pug' is at the point where the Company's line met the Harborne branch. This locomotive was subsequently preserved. *Howard Turvey.*

The final steam locomotives to act regularly as New Street pilots on the Western Lines side were Stanier Class '3' 2-6-2 tanks. 40129 is standing with parcels vans at Platform 1A Birmingham New Street on 11 July 1959. *Michael Mensing.*

The 4.13am was newspapers from London and he would split at New Street. The first two carriages went to Stafford, the next two went to Walsall, and the others stopped in New Street for unloading and went back empty to Vauxhall. (RL).

A regular empty newspaper train also operated from New Street via Marton Junction to Rugby, although this appears to have ended by the 1950s.

THE NEW STREET PILOTS

Given its size, New Street needed engines on constant standby to shunt carriages, help with empty stock movements and move parcels or freight wagons. Because New Street had developed as a joint station, handling trains from the Midland Railway and the London and North Western Railway, both companies supplied locomotives to look after operations, an approach which continued into both LMS and BR days. Consequently, Saltley and Bournville provided the pilots on the Midland side of the station, whilst Monument Lane normally assumed full responsibility for the Western Lines, providing two locomotives, one for each end of the station.

The actual duties varied, in that for the north (Wolverhampton) end, men and locos could be called upon to pilot down expresses as far as Dudley Port or Wolverhampton to help them over the more difficult route. At the south end there were no such requirements, with most of the work taking place in the confines of New Street, interspersed with an occasional trip to Vauxhall Carriage sidings.

Because of the differing needs, the north end bank engines were passenger locomotives, whilst at the south end they were goods engines. In order to meet the demands of the work, both pilot locomotives normally worked almost continuously over a 24 hour period, with the exception of a daily trip to the shed for coaling and watering around mid day. Each locomotive would make the short trip to the shed separately and the other would cover.

With regard to driving and firing arrangements, contrasting levels of experience applied. For the south end shunt the firemen were men working their way up through the links. At the north end passed firemen were employed who would therefore be on hand at New Street to fill in on a driving turn at short notice. During summer months, though, passed firemen would more often be required for driving duties on seasonal extras, reducing their availability for the pilots. The north end drivers were senior men in their own link. They were former top link men who wished to give up the rigours of the main line and they could move into the link when a vacancy arose.

In early days the duties fell to Saddle Tanks, betraying their age by the lack of protection afforded to crews. Later, ex LNW 'Special Tanks' and 'Box Tanks' took their turn, but the classes that would become most associated with the duties as the 20th Century progressed were ex LNW 0-6-2 tank engines, consisting of 'Watford Tanks' for the north end, and 'Coal Tanks' for the south end. Other classes were also called on to help out should the designated locomotive be unavailable, including tender locomotives such as 'Cauliflowers', '2F' 0-6-0s, '4Fs' and even Compounds.

Finally, three Stanier Class '3' 2-6-2 tank locos, 40108, 40118 and 40129 shared the duties before diesel shunters took over towards the end of 1960.

5

MONUMENT LANE ENGINES

Monument Lane provided locomotives for main line and local passenger workings together with local goods traffic, so the shed had a mix of engine classes. In practice the freight locomotives were not always the most modern of designs but for the local passenger turns appropriate locomotives were normally provided so that new examples of tank classes found their way to Monument Lane, in keeping with the shed's need to power heavily loaded suburban trains around the West Midlands.

However, for main line workings the shed never possessed the more powerful engines after the Victorian era. Thus, when the later LNW express locomotives were in production it would be the 'Experiments', 'Precursors', 'Prince of Wales' and 'George V' classes that were allocated to the shed rather than the larger 'Claughtons'. The Post Grouping period saw that trend continue, with LMS Compounds playing a major role and the practice continued with the introduction of William Stanier's classes. Indeed, of his tender locomotive designs only 'Black 5s' were ever allocated to Monument Lane, with not even a 'Jubilee' featuring. Moreover, following nationalisation the shed never received a single BR design steam locomotive, although one or two Stanier Class '5s' produced after 1948 with additional experimental features did work from the shed.

Modern steam locomotives may have been conspicuous by their absence but the shed did receive some brand new diesel multiple units. It was therefore the first shed in the West Midlands to operate the new units, which were ultimately joined by a mix of diesel shunting engines.

STEAM LOCOMOTIVES
The 19th Century
During the early days of the shed Trevithick single wheelers were based at Monument Lane. By the mid to late 1870s the allocation included half a

dozen new 'Samson' class 2-4-0s. They included 2155 *Liver*, 2157 *Unicorn*, 2158 *Serpent*, 2153 *Isis*, 2154 *Loadstone* and 2156 *Sphinx*. Also present was 852 *Kestrel*. Amongst the last to appear, in 1879, *Kestrel* was withdrawn in 1894. Towards the latter part of the 19th Century the shed boasted a number of 6 ft 'Jumbos', including 752 *Glow-worm*, 1164 *Odin*, 285 *Phalaris* and 852 *Kestrel*. Other tender locomotives included McConnell 'Bloomers' 894 *Trentham* and 895 *Torch*, together with 'Newton' 2-4-0s 1523 *Marlborough* and 1525 *Abercrombie* from a class that appeared in the latter half of the 1860s and early 1870s. On 30 June 1896 there were seven Whitworth '6 foots' allocated to the shed.

Tank engines in those early days included Webb 2-4-0s, such as 2250 and 2251, Crewe Goods No 337, Saddle Tank 946 and St Helens Railway *WHITE RAVEN*, as rebuilt as a 2-4-0 and renumbered 1818. In addition the shed possessed a number of 0-6-0 goods engines.

The Edwardian Era

From the late Victorian and Edwardian period came the 0-6-2 'Watford Tanks' and 'Coal Tanks' that would be long associated with the shed, together with George Whale's express passenger 4-4-2 tank engines, both of which found regular employment on Birmingham area services. They were accompanied during the years leading up to World War I by 'Experiments', including 507 *Sarmatian* and 1455 *Herefordshire*. Main line services were also hauled by 'Precursors', including 2 *Simoon*, 184 *Havelock* and 1312 *Ionic*, together with 'Prince of Wales' and 'George V' classes.

The 1920s and the coming of the Compounds

By the mid 1920s the depot had a mix of LNWR types of both passenger and freight. They included 'Prince of Wales' 2417 *Atlas*, 2021 *Wolvreing*, 637 *Thomas Gray*, 362 *Robert Southey*, 522 *Stentor*, 740 and 1408, 'George Vs' 1059 *Lord Loch*, 1559 *Drake*, 1218 and 404 *Eclipse*. The 'Precursors' included 7 *Titan* and 1577 *Dunrobin*.

The tank engines were a mix of types, with 'Watford Tanks' 4, 14, 78, 741, 1095, 2211 and 2382, '5'6"' 2-4-2Ts, including 1389 and 2264, which acted as station pilots at the north end of New Street. At the south end would be a 'Special' 0-6-0 saddle tank, selected from 3327, 3615 and 3659. There were also 0-6-0 saddle tanks (known to some as 'Box Tanks' or 'Aircraft Carriers') at the shed, one of which was 3197. The passenger tanks included 4-4-2 'Precursors', which tended to work the heavier local services, including 111, 1219, 803, 1714, 527, 528 and 834. Also present were 'Prince' 4-6-2 tanks 809, 841, 944, 962, 1797 and 2670.

Following the Grouping, Midland Railway influences began to appear on the former LNW lines as men with a Midland background took on many of the senior positions affecting locomotive practices in the newly formed London Midland and Scottish Railway. Of particular note was the introduction of a further series of Compound 4-4-0s, a number of which were sent to Monument Lane, including some virtually fresh from construction. The first to arrive was 1157, during week ending 24 October 1925. Others quickly followed so that 1172, 1174, 1175 and 1177 were on the shed's stock list by the end of February 1926. The 'George V' and 'Prince of Wales' survived to work alongside the Compounds but the days of the 'Precursors' were almost over at Monument Lane.

By the late 1920s the freight locomotives were very much the same as they had been for some years, comprising three tender classes and three tank engine classes. The tender locomotives were 0-6-0 'Coal Engines', 0-6-0 'Cauliflowers' and' Whale's 4-6-0 '4Fs', whilst the tank engines were made up of 'Coal Tanks', 'Special Tanks' and a small number of 0-6-0 'Box Tanks'. Right at the end of the decade the number of Box Tanks reduced to one and in return the shed did receive two much newer replacements in the form of LMS 'Jinties' 16450 and 16451.

The 1930s. New 'Black 5s' – and some farewells

The 1930s saw great changes on the locomotive front at Monument Lane. It was a decade when many of the older passenger classes departed for the last time and brand new locomotives of both tender and tank variety came to take their place. In most cases, though, the freight locomotives continued to originate from the Victorian period. The 0-6-0 'Coal Engines', for example, included some which were amongst the oldest of the class, originating from 1873.

Gradually during the early years of the 1930s the shed lost its 'Coal Engines', 'Cauliflowers' and 4-6-0s only for them to be replaced by engines that were just as old. They were six ex-Midland Railway Johnson '2F' 0-6-0s, 3005-3010, which arrived from Westhouses and Toton sheds in the East Midlands during week ending 6 July 1932. Despite their age they proved to be long lasting and 3005, 3006 and 3007 had long associations with the shed, with 3006 – later 58178 – remaining until withdrawn in 1959. One 'Coal Engine', 28261, returned briefly in 1936 and that proved to be the end of the shed's association with that class.

During 1934 the shed also received its first LMS built '4F' 0-6-0, in the form of 4490. The '4F' remained for only a short period, although it would have a much longer association with the shed in the 1950s, and the number of '4Fs' never exceeded a single example before 1940.

Then the ex LNW passenger locomotives began to leave for the last time. In November 1936 the last 'George V' at the shed, 5344 *Newcomen*, transferred to Birkenhead and just a few weeks later the final 'Prince of Wales', 25673 *Lusitania*, departed. *Lusitania* had been the sole surviving 'Prince of Wales' at Monument Lane for some twelve months and its departure also marked another milestone – never again would a named locomotive be allocated to the depot.

Next it was the turn of the 'Precursor Tanks'. By the dawn of 1935 only 6821 and 6822 could still be found 'on shed'. Actually, another, 6782, arrived at the very end of 1936 but that event did not swell the numbers, as it coincided with the withdrawal of 6821. Three months later 6822 suffered a similar fate, leaving 6782 as the final example until August 1937 when it transferred to Rugby.

So what was happening to replace those veterans? Initially the shed received three LMS 'Crabs'. Their stay was a brief one and they were replaced by two Stanier 2-6-0s, 13280 (later 2980) and 13282 (2982), both barely two years old. 13282 remained for only three months but 13273 (2973) arrived later in the year. Both departed in March 1937 before returning for the summer months, but in September of 1937 they finally moved on.

In 1936, though, brand new engines began to arrive, in the form of Stanier Class '4' 2-6-4 tanks. First to arrive, in June 1936, was 2449, to be followed at various intervals over the next nine months by 2450, 2451, 2487, 2567 and 2579.

Finally came the 'super power', at least in Monument Lane terms, when 'Black 5' 5131 travelled down from Crewe North during March 1936. Towards the end of the same year, classmates 5245 and 5257 came brand new, with a similarly gleaming 5301 following very early in 1937. Generally speaking there would normally be five or six Class '5s' at the shed during the late 1930s.

On the freight locomotive front, the depot also saw a number of ex LNW 0-8-0s on the scene in the mid 1930s of both 'G1' and 'G2a' classes. 'G2a' 9042 was at the depot at the beginning of 1935 and a further four examples arrived for varying periods between 1937 and 1940 before the last example, 9050, departed in August 1940.

The Midland Railway was also represented by a small number of '3F' 0-6-0 tanks, with both 1777 and 1818 present during the 1930s. They left in early 1937 but were replaced by 1726 and 1727. 1726, which still bore spring balance safety valves on its dome, was the last example to leave, in April 1940.

The War Years

The war years were a period when the shed saw a definite backward step in terms of its principal locomotive power, as it would lose all of its Class '5' 4-6-0s from March 1941 and it would be five years before the shed had another Class '5' to call its own. Thus, when Monument Lane engines were required for main line work, it fell to the Compounds of the tender classes, with five or six to be found on the strength. The only exception occurred when a couple of ex Midland '2P' 4-4-0s, 515 and 539, arrived in June 1942. Of the two, 515 remained only briefly but 539 worked from the shed for a year before moving to Longsight.

The Compounds remained, though, with a dozen different examples gracing the shed between 1940 and the end of the war. The number allocated varied, falling to three at times, whereas during the latter part of 1946 there were nine Compounds at Monument Lane, meaning that the class comprised over one quarter of all locomotives there. The longest to stay was 1111 (from January 1942 right through to September 1950).

The early years of the war also the arrival of three 'Special' tanks, 27351, 27353 and 27370, at various stages during 1939 and 1940. By then over 60 years old, all three had departed for the scrapyard by the end of 1940. Of more modern vintage were three Fowler '3P' 2-6-2 tanks which arrived during the early 1940s. They left just before nationalisation and were replaced by more powerful Fairburn Class '4' 2-6-4 tanks, 42262, 42263, 42264, 42265, 42267 and 42677. The Fairburn tanks therefore operated alongside Stanier examples of similar power classification.

THE POST NATIONALISATION SCENE

With the dawn of nationalisation the depot had an allocation of thirty one locomotives, consisting of a mix of examples with LNW origins, ex Midland freight locomotives and just over half of which were built by the LMS.

There was increasing movement amongst the ex LNW 0-6-2 tank locomotives and eleven of the fifteen 'Watford Tanks' that survived into nationalisation saw service at Monument Lane before the last example was withdrawn in 1953. Eight Webb 'Coal Tanks' also spent parts of their last years at the shed. They, like the Watford Tanks', could be found fussing around New Street station in the post nationalisation era. In the late 1940s and early 1950s the turnover of both classes was high, but as one old soldier faded away another arrived to take its place. One of the 'Coal Tanks', 58916, had received extended side tanks to increase water capacity in order to work local passenger services in the Wirral.

The shed actually received a brand new Ivatt Class 2 tank, 41214, in the Autumn of 1948 and it immediately took up duty as New Street south end station pilot. However, within six weeks the 2-6-2T had moved on – and was replaced by two Coal Tanks!

Ex-Midland Railway 2Fs remained and the shed also acquired a couple of 'Cauliflowers', 58427 and 58429. They worked alongside ex LMS '4F' 0-6-0s whilst in 1949, 43231, a Johnson '3F' 0-6-0, arrived for what was to prove a lengthy stay.

In November 1949 the number of Coal Tanks increased when 58928 transferred from Bletchley. That locomotive became something of a local celebrity when the shed staff gave it the unofficial name *Chipper*, after a cartoon dog that appeared in the *Evening Despatch* newspaper. As a result, when *Chipper* was withdrawn its demise was actually reported in the *Evening Despatch*. Withdrawal occurred during the week ending 27 January 1951, but 58900 was despatched from Sutton Oak as a replacement, first appearing during February 1951.

At the end of September 1950, coinciding with the end of summer services, the shed's four Compounds departed, leaving the shed without a 4-4-0 for the first time since the 19th century. The situation was redressed the following July, however, when four newcomers transferred in, 40926, 40933, 40936 and 41090. Of the new arrivals, 40936 was something of a celebrity, having been paired with an experimental high sided tender back in June 1935.

1950 also proved of interest when former Lancashire & Yorkshire 'Pug' 51218 transferred from Preston in September. That move occurred in order to help out the brewery company Mitchells and Butler's, whose own locomotives were unavailable. Its duties completed by mid September, 51218 departed for Crewe South.

With regard to the Class '5s', the period from 1952 to 1956 was one of the most settled of all the years after nationalisation, with the same three members of the class remaining constantly at the shed, 45390, 45051 and 44942. Of those, 44942 was a member of the class with a self cleaning firebox and came to the shed by special request to cover the 12.10pm to Manchester London Road. On arrival at Manchester the locomotive remained at London Road, where there was a pit for basic servicing. The self cleaning firebox therefore made servicing easier.

During 1953 the shed loaned Class '5' 45051 to the Southern Region for one month during May 1953 to help out when the 'Merchant Navies' were temporarily withdrawn for remedial work to be undertaken following the derailment of one member of the class.

1954 saw a major change in the locomotives working on the New Street pilots. In April of that year 58900 ended a three year association with Monument Lane and was transferred to Swansea. It was not the end for the class as an immediate replacement arrived in the form of 58903. For 58903 there would be a final burst of glory, when she found herself on passenger duties on June 1st and 2nd hauling a Stephenson Locomotive Society special around parts of Birmingham. Within a fortnight, though, 58903 was withdrawn, an event of particular significance as it ended the depot's allocation of locomotives originating from the London and North Western Railway Company.

It was to Stanier Class '3' 2-6-2 tank locomotives that the shed turned for its pilot duties, with three on the strength by September 1954, 40108, 40118 and 40129. It was also during 1954 that another exchange of tank locomotives took place. Four of the Fairburn examples, 42262, 42263, 42264 and 42265 transferred to Greenock and the Scottish depot sent replacements in the form of Fowler engines 42419, 42420, 42421 and 42422. During January 1954 the high sided tender transferred from 40936 to 40933.

In 1955 a push pull service was introduced on certain off peak services on the Sutton Coldfield and Four Oaks services. As a result, three Ivatt 2-6-2 tank locomotives, 41223, 41224 and 41320 arrived in April of that year at Monument Lane.

DIESELISATION ARRIVES

The re-vamping of Lichfield services caused by the arrival of the diesel multiple units led to a reshuffle amongst the shed's passenger locomotive contingent. Firstly, all three of the 'Black 5s', 44942, 45051 and 45390 were transferred out in March and April 1956. They were not replaced for several months so the Compounds were nominally once again left to fly the flag as the sole passenger tender locos at 3E. In reality that was not the case, as all three were in store by mid May, where they stayed until the summer of 1957. It was not as though they were all in a run down condition, as 40936 underwent a heavy general repair in October 1955 but was placed in store in March 1956. The engine record card shows that it completed just 283 miles in 1956, despite being virtually ex works!

As a result, Monument Lane had no tender passenger locomotives to work its more prestigious services, a situation that was addressed by using engines from other sheds on the services. The tank locomotives actually changed type in March 1956 when the Fowler engines, 42419, 42420 and 42421, were replaced by Stanier 2-6-4 examples 42552, 42601 and 42558.

Stanier Class '5s' returned to the shed in the form of 45034 and 45308 during week ending 3 November 1956. In addition, a further influx throughout 1957 meant that by the end of that year there were seven examples allocated to Monument Lane, primarily to help with additional work to London, although they also provided a broad hint that the days of the Compounds were numbered. To confirm the point, 40933 departed for Gloucester in December, whilst 41090 moved to the same shed in February. However, 41168 returned to the strength at Monument Lane in June 1958.

At the same time two '4Fs' arrived from Walsall when that shed closed to steam. They were 44115 and 44444. The only locomotive in the BR era to have the same five numerals, legend has it that 44444 caused one misunderstanding when a member of the shed staff was asked to "oil all the 4s" – and promptly oiled every '4F' on shed.

The shed did effectively lose one of its '4Fs' in 1958. One evening 44506 was undergoing a routine check by one of the fitters and it appears that the regulator was left open. When it was subsequently lit up it was left unattended and ran away in the shed yard, hitting one of the stop blocks and suffering extensive front end damage. It was immediately placed into store where it remained for over two years before it was withdrawn.

There was quite a turnover of Class '5s' in the late 1950s but the arrival of 44807, 45038 and 45052 in September 1958 coincided with storage for the two remaining Compounds, 40936 and 41168, for the last time. The numbers of Johnson '2F' 0-6-0s also reduced, falling to three in 1957, a reduction that was compensated for by the arrival of three 'Jinties', 47474, 47494 and 47561, all of which were transferred to the shed during October. The day of the Johnson veterans was far from over, though, and they would labour between the various goods yards for some time to come.

The onset of warmer weather saw the usual changeover of Class '5s' but the newcomers were of particular interest that year. They included 44760 and 44766, both fitted with Timken roller bearings. 44766 also included a double chimney amongst its fittings.

The penultimate round of Class '5' movement began at the end of April 1960 and the new arrivals included 44686, which arrived during week ending 30 April but departed shortly afterwards during the week ending 14 May 1960. 44686 was another non standard variant of the class, with Caprotti valve gear and Skefko roller bearings, and the most modern locomotive of the post nationalisation era to be allocated to the shed. One record of its activities at the shed has survived, showing that it worked the 5.15am parcels from New Street to Rugby on 26 April. All of the Class '5's had moved elsewhere by the end of October and none would return until the Summer of 1961. The departure of the Class '5s' did not completely take away passenger tender locomotives. Parked on the far side of the shed yard, chimneys sacked and protected from the winter rains and snows, were the two Compounds, 40936 and 41168.

From 14 November 1960 the winds of change began to blow even more strongly when the shed gained its first diesel shunters. That led to a reduction in the number of '4F' 0-6-0s, with the notable loss of two long stay examples. 44057, resident throughout the BR era, moved on to Northampton and 44490 left during the same November week for Buxton. Another '4F' also departed, although on this occasion for the breaker's yard when 44506 was finally hauled away after more than two years of inactivity.

The Summer timetable for 1961 began in June, a signal for the Stanier Class '5s' to return. Four representatives arrived but their return, though, was a brief one and the final member of the class, 45071, set off north for Speke Junction at the end of October.

Time was also running out for the Johnson '2Fs'. Their ranks were reduced to four when 58123 departed for Bescot at the end of March and the withdrawal of 58271 followed at the end of May. Of the two remaining Johnsons, 58135 was withdrawn in September 1961 but 58185 was re-allocated to Bescot during the last week of December, although the 0-6-0 was still to be found in the shed yard in January 1962.

Despite ongoing withdrawals of other classes, the two Compounds, 40936 and 41168, remained officially in service at the dawn of 1961. In reality neither had made any revenue earning contribution since 1958. First to go was 40936, withdrawn during January. However, 41168 remained on the books until week ending 8 July 1961, becoming the last survivor of its class.

The depot also lost its Stanier '3Ps' when 40118 and 40129 were withdrawn in November and October respectively, made redundant by the diesel shunters which could now be found at New Street on pilot and banking duties.

Monument Lane officially closed to steam on 10 February 1962. Just eight engines remained to be transferred out, 42267, 42488, 42544, 44444, 44514, 47341, 47474 and 47494. All were despatched to Aston with the exception of 42544, which returned to Rugby from where it was on loan. Of the final survivors, special mention should be made of 44514, which had spent the entire post nationalisation period at the shed, moving to Monument Lane in May 1942.

VISITING LOCOMOTIVES

As with most sheds, Monument Lane men used locomotives from 'foreign' sheds. Summer and relief work in particular placed a heavy burden on the shed's limited stud of passenger locomotives, leading to a need to borrow engines from other depots, such as Aston, Bushbury and Crewe. Moreover, with its proximity to New Street, servicing of visiting locomotives was an essential element of the depot's work.

In the post nationalisation era an occasional 'Britannia' would appear in the shed yard. 'Britannias' had to be turned carefully as locomotives on the turntable passed close to the adjacent stores' wall on their circuit – so close that the ladder on the back of the 'Britannia' tender would catch the down pipe from the guttering and knock it off the wall, so it had to be smokebox first!

There are also records of 'Clans' appearing at Monument Lane or on Monument Lane duties. During running in working, 72003 *Clan Fraser* spent an evening on shed on 30 January 1952 after a fault developed. The men also worked 72006 *Clan Mackenzie* to London – when again a fault developed!

The shed also shared duties with Burton depot and Burton Class '2' 4-4-0s came to Monument Lane for servicing. One regular engine was 40633, which was fitted with a Dabeg water feed pump, and which, in the post war years, did two out and back trips from Burton to New Street. It was normally the habit to leave it in a siding by the signalbox before it made its return journey in the afternoon. The shed could also call on Bescot, as the lead shed in the district, to supply locos when shortages occurred. Two regulars at one time were Stanier Class '5' 44914, which could often be seen working to London, and 'Crab' 2-6-0 42929.

In 1954 Monument Lane paid host to two celebrities, which arrived in connection with events to mark the centenary of New Street station. The first was the retired LNW 'Jumbo' *Hardwicke*, which was hauled dead to Monument Lane from its home at Crewe Works. The second was Stanier Pacific 46235 *City of Birmingham*, which was actually lit up at the shed after its time on display at New Street.

'Black 5s' 45495 and 44966 spent around one week on shed in 1955 being prepared for Royal Train duties, which fell to Monument Lane men to work. When they finally moved off the shed on 3 November their pristine condition owed much to the shed's cleaning staff and the painting skills of Foreman's Assistant Jack Middleton.

Rarities from other sheds were a possibility, such as Holbeck's 45597 *Barbados* on Easter Monday 1953. Also of interest was the occasion when three Eastern Region engines, consisting of 'B17' 61663 and 'B1s' 61384 and 61227, worked a football special conveying Tottenham Hotspur supporters for an FA Cup semi final tie at Villa Park and came to the shed for servicing. 'B1s' would become more regular visitors on through workings from the Eastern Region as the 1950s progressed.

At Christmas the shed borrowed 'Super Ds' for postal mails from New Street to Monument Lane, whilst on one occasion a Riddles 'Austerity' turned up light from Bescot. Even rarer were '9F' 2-10-0s, with no known sightings of one on the shed.

Of those locomotives from other sheds on which the men worked, 'Black 5' 45324 is recalled with particular fondness by Brian Clarke as a first class engine to fire. At the other extreme, Bushbury's Jubilee 45688 *Polyphemus* was often an unwelcome sight as it had a reputation as a poor steamer.

THE DIESELS

Monument Lane's diesel allocation consisted of diesel multiple units from 1956 and a small number of diesel shunters, which began to arrive in November 1960. The first diesel multiple units were Derby Lightweight units, most of which reached the shed in February and March 1956. The power cars were numbered from M79127 to M79134, M79145 to M79149 and M79169 to M79170. The Lightweight units remained at Monument Lane throughout 1957 and into the early months of 1958. However, improvements were on the horizon in the shape of the much sturdier three car Metropolitan Cammell units, which would later become Class '101s'. The last day when the 79xxx series monopolised services was 31 May 1958 and from 2 June the Metropolitan Cammell units took over. The power cars fell in the series M50303 to M50338.

From November 1958 Metropolitan Cammell 2 car units were also allocated to the shed in the series M51174 to M51191 and at one stage there were 18 three car sets and 14 two car sets at the shed. The two car Metropolitan Cammell units remained at the shed until the early months of 1965, when they were replaced by two car units built by the Gloucester Railway Carriage and Wagon Company numbered from M50348 to M50357. The Gloucester units in turn stayed at the shed until April and May 1966 when they were replaced by three car units from the Birmingham Railway Carriage and Works Company, including M50439 – M50440, M50442 – M50451, M50491 – M50492 and M50494 to M50503. From time to time other types would be allocated to the shed for short periods, including Cravens and Derby Works units.

During the latter part of 1966 an exchange of sets took place involving the former Western Region units based at Tyseley. The DMUs were not formally transferred but it did lead to different types arriving at Monument Lane depot for servicing.

DIESEL SHUNTERS

Between November 1960 and the closure of the shed in March 1967 three different types of diesel shunter worked from Monument Lane. The first to arrive were three 0-6-0s which became Class '08s', D3839, D3840 and D3841 accompanied by an older type, 12092, ultimately Class '11'. In May 1961 D2387 (later Class '03') came to the shed and that would be followed by classmates D2395 and D2396 in August 1961 and finally D2386 in November 1961. Another Class '11', 12071, came to the shed in September 1961 and the contingent was completed by D3089 in January 1961 and D3956 in September 1964, whose arrival came shortly after D2396 left.

D2396 was transferred to the Western Region, providing Brian Clarke with a pilot working from Monument Lane to the Western Region via Bordesley Junction. There he handed over control before enjoying a trip through Birmingham's Snow Hill station and leaving the shunter at Hockley station and making his way back to the shed. Then D3956 left for Tyseley in February 1966 and two of the '03s' left in early 1967. The remaining shunters, D3089, D3839, D3840, D3841, 12071 and 12092 stayed until the shed closed in March 1967.

6

THE MEN

THE VICTORIAN ERA

Given that Monument Lane was one of the smaller sheds on the London and North Western Railway it is not surprising that some of the men saw it as a stepping stone to greater things. Amongst those to move on were Assistant Foreman Stilton, who transferred to Derby in November 1877, and Charles Clench, Under Foreman, who received approval for a move to Stafford in January 1883. Despite six years elapsing between the two moves both men were on a weekly wage of two pounds five shillings (£2.25).

Wages had improved by May 1898 when E E Richardson – yet another Assistant Foreman – moved to the post of Locomotive Foreman at Northampton and an annual salary of £160. He was 54 at the time of his move.

By the early years of the 20th Century the Assistant Foreman was F H Miller. Born in 1863, F Miller entered the service of the LNWR in December 1877 and received a salary of £150 per annum from October 1901. Other men at the shed in its earlier years included George Welletts, who was the Foreman in the mid 1880s, and William King, who was employed as a fitter for many years.

Amongst its footplate crews were men who had moved from other parts of the country. Henry Quick originated from Linslade in Buckinghamshire and, after spending over 20 years at the shed, returned to his home town as a stationary engine driver. From Oxfordshire came Thomas Gardner, whose footplate career ended in 1884 when he was dismissed for entering Sutton Coldfield station at excessive speed and he demolished the buffer stops. At that time Sutton Coldfield was still the last station on the line. He did apply for re-employment by the company and he was allowed to work as a stoker at one of the LNWR's hydraulic pumping establishments.

Two of the Monument Lane Compounds, 41116 and 41111, stand at the head of a local working at New Street on Saturday 2 July 1949. *Initial Photographics/R J Buckley.*

Monument Lane engines and men regularly worked to North Wales and the North West of England on Summer Saturdays. Compound 41163 is leaving Crewe station on 8 August 1953 with the 3.40pm from Blackpool to New Street, which was the return working of the 9am from New Street to Blackpool. *H C Casserley.*

Members of the Birmingham Locomotive Club found Monument Lane's '4F' 44057 at the head of their train for a railtour which included the Stratford and Midland Joint Railway as part of the itinerary on 14 July 1951. Later in the tour 44057 has paused at Olney, on the Midland Railway branch from Bedford to Northampton. *T J Edgington*.

Even further off the beaten track, 45051 displays its 3E shedplate at the most unlikely of locations – London's Waterloo station. At this time the 'Black 5' was on loan to the Southern Region to help out during a locomotive shortage brought about by the temporary withdrawal of the entire 'Merchant Navy' class. *RC Riley/Transport Treasury*.

The carriage shed can be seen just beyond Monument Lane station. To the right is the Class '4' tank engaged on shunting duties, and a Class '5' awaits a main line working. To the left in the shed is English Electric diesel 10800, which will work the 3.55pm from New Street as far as Peterborough. Another Class '5' approaches on a freight train. The date is 27 June 1955, and plans to convert the building to a Diesel Shed are well underway. *D J Norton.*

The carriage shed pilot, a 2-6-4 tank, undertakes some shunting around 1950. *Howard Turvey.*

Class '2P' 40513 is setting out from Derby with brand new Derby Lightweight unit M79125 destined for Monument Lane on 29 March 1956. *R J Buckley/Initial Photographics.*

It is the first month of Diesel operation and two twin car 'Derby Lightweight' units arrive at Witton station on the 1.2pm New Street to Rugeley (Trent Valley) on 14 March 1956. *Michael Mensing.*

A lengthy eight 2 car 'Derby Lightweight' DMU set arriving at Birmingham New Street from the Diesel Shed on 7 May 1957. The various sets will split, with the first 6 cars forming the 5.15pm to Lichfield, the 2nd car set will work the 5.20pm to Lichfield and the last 4 cars will await a later set to join and form the 5.42pm to Four Oaks. On the left one of the shed's Class '3' Stanier tanks acts as station pilot. *Michael Mensing.*

The 'Derby Lightweights' lasted at Monument Lane until May 1958, when they were replaced by Metropolitan Cammell units. Two 3 car Metropolitan Cammell DMUs are arriving at Gravelly Hill station on the 5.30pm Lichfield (Trent Valley) to New Street service on 23 August 1958. *Michael Mensing.*

The DMUs ventured further afield than Monument Lane's tank engines, with Peterborough becoming a regular destination. A 3 car Metropolitan Cammell set is approaching Peterborough East with the 8.50am from New Street on 6 June 1960. *Michael Mensing.*

Steam power continued from Monument Lane into the early 1960s. Class '5' 45111 stands at Birmingham New Street with the empty stock of a City of Birmingham Holiday Express working from Alton Towers, on 28 July 1960. A number of the Holiday Express trains fell to the shed, with different locations providing the destination over the period of a week. Whenever possible, the locomotives were well turned out for these workings. *Michael Mensing.*

18 March 1959 saw the supporters of Third Division Norwich City descend on Birmingham for an FA Cup tie. Several football excursions worked through to Birmingham behind 'B1' locomotives, with Monument Lane men taking over at Rugby. Here is one such train, passing Stechford in the Birmingham suburbs behind 61204. *Michael Mensing.*

It is 18 February 1961 and diesel shunters have taken over station pilot work at New Street. D3840 is shunting a wagon into the siding at the end of Platform 6. *Michael Mensing.*

The station pilot duties at New Street were shared between what became Class '08' and Class '03' shunters. One of the latter, D2395, is attached to parcels vans at New Street on Sunday 12 September 1965. *Michael Mensing.*

This 1959 scene shows the shed with a range of steam locomotives present. They include, from the right, ex Midland Railway Class '4F', 43973, Rugby Class '5' 44863, a Jubilee, a 2-6-4 tank and two Class '5s', the one to the left being Crewe North's 44682. *R S Carpenter Collection.*

In 1961 rumours began to circulate that the shed would close in the Summer of that year. Scenes such as this, with rows of stored locomotives, including 40936 and 44506, and little other activity, would have supported that view but the shed remained open throughout the year. *H H Bleads/courtesy Colin Bleads.*

Driver Howard Stanley 'oils' Compound 41168 on 4 August 1960. By then, the Compound had been stored for almost 2 years and would have required considerably more oil than Howard has available in his can before it became serviceable! 41168 was not withdrawn until week ending 7 July 1961, although it remained inactive until that date. *F A Wycherley.*

Stanier Class '5' 45111 is at Stockport Edgeley engine shed on 20 June 1960. It was rare for Monument Lane engines to appear at this shed but this manoeuvre is taking place at a time when Manchester London Road was closed for electrification work to take place. Consequently, Monument Lane engines came off the 12.10pm from New Street at Stockport, which then worked forward to Manchester Victoria with a local engine. The engine bears a 3E shedplate but this was actually the date from which the shed code changed to 21E. *D Forsyth/P Chancellor collection.*

Monument Lane Class '5' 45052 approaches Peterborough East on 25 July 1959 with the 7.04am from Birmingham to Clacton. The locomotive, crewed by Rugby men, worked through to Ely before returning home with the 11.23am from Clacton to Birmingham. *D Ovenden/P Chancellor collection.*

Two 3 car Metropolitan Cammell units are arriving at New Street to form the 5.20pm service to Lichfield (City). Alongside is Fairburn tank 42267 waiting to form the 5.48pm to Rugby Midland, a service which still retained regular steam haulage at this time despite the growing involvement of DMUs on local suburban services. The date is 28 March 1961. *Michael Mensing.*

Monument Lane driver Frank Ward is at the controls of D5061 with the 3.58pm from New Street to Yarmouth as it passes a three car and a two car DMU set arriving at Coventry with the 4.10pm Rugby Midland to New Street on 25 February 1961. *Michael Mensing.*

Class '5' 45324 awaiting departure at New Street with the 3.55pm to the East Coast on 29 July 1961. In the view of Brian Clarke this was the finest of all the 'Black 5s' on which he worked, although it was never allocated to 3E. Here it is a Rugby engine but Monument Lane men are on the footplate and will work through to Rugby. *D Forsyth/P Chancellor collection.*

At the other extreme, Bushbury's Jubilee 45688 *Polyphemus* was not a welcome sight as it had a reputation as an indifferent steamer. Here it is at Rugby belying its reputation with steam to spare when working the 11.55 from Wolverhampton Low Level to London Euston on 27 July 1954. Monument Lane men are not involved on this occasion but this is one of the services on which they regularly assisted. *Roger Shenton.*

The shed on 7 October 1962, eight months after closure to steam and with an overgrown and empty 'Promenade'. *R S Carpenter Collection.*

Although steam has left the site, the few diesel shunters allocated to the shed would return at weekends and DMUs visited for certain repairs to be carried out. A view of the entrance to the shed on Sunday 7 October 1962. *R S Carpenter Collection.*

The diesel shed, though, has only a single occupant on the same day. *R S Carpenter Collection*.

Left: On 3 November 1955 Vic Blumfield (left) and Roy Judge are ready to work the Royal Train from Stechford in Birmingham to London. This was the first occasion on which a telephone was available on the locomotive for a Royal Train duty, enabling the Inspector to travel in the first carriage rather than on the footplate. *Roy Judge collection*. Right: Doug Piggin is alongside one of the shed's long standing '4Fs'.

Left: Frank Ward poses alongside one of the shed's '4Fs', 44057. Frank's career began at Aston shed and he moved to Monument Lane in 1952. His driving career ranged from Midland Railway freight engines built in the 1870s to Inter City High Speed Trains produced in the 1970s. *Frank Ward collection.* Right: Brian Clarke is on cleaning duties at the shed. Brian started at Monument Lane in 1951 and remained there until closure in 1967. He remained with BR until the 1990s, retiring as Depot Manager at New Street. He can be heard providing expert input on two Railscene videos. *Brian Clarke collection.*

Ray Gower is on 40108, one of the New Street bank engines. Ray's career began on the Midland Railway at Bromsgrove around the time of World War I. He moved to Birmingham and became a top link driver at Monument Lane. He ended his days in the bank link and it is believed that this photograph was taken on Ray's last day of service sometime in the late 1950s and the only thing missing from this superb image of Ray is his clay pipe. *Birmingham Post and Mail.*

The men, mostly trainee guards, gather alongside one of the new diesel railcars. In the cab of the unit is diesel instructor Hywel ('Taffy') Hughes and on the far right is Albert Colley, who worked at the diesel shed. *Margaret Colley collection.*

An electric locomotive sweeps past to demonstrate that there is no future for steam power and the shed is in the final stages of demolition in 1968. *David Johnson.*

Prominent amongst those on the footplate around the dawn of the 20th Century was William Henry Woods. William Woods' career began on 9 February 1871 in the Curzon Street stores before he moved to Monument Lane as a fireman in 1879. He became a driver at the time when New Street was being enlarged on the Midland side, as he had charge of trains removing debris from the site to Soho. He was similarly employed on construction of the Perry Barr loop in 1887.

After working for several years on local passenger and goods trains, in 1890 he piloted express goods services between Birmingham, Manchester and Liverpool, as well as working passenger services to the North Wales coast. He was then one of three Birmingham drivers selected for the launch of the two hour 35 minute expresses in 1900 and he also drove the two hour expresses when they were introduced, remaining on those trains for 23 years. When he retired in 1928, at the age of 70, he claimed to have a longer record of service than any other railway servant in the country, as he had achieved a total of 58 years railway service, of which 51 were spent on the footplate.

Another driver was Edward Clemson. During one his trips, on a freight to Wichnor Junction, his fireman George Durham fell from the footplate and was killed. At the subsequent inquest the jury recommended that handrails should be fitted to locomotives. Another death occurred on 28 December 1899 when Thomas Bench was caught between two engines.

MEN OF THE 1920s AND 1930s

During the 1920s men who would become top link drivers in later years arrived at Monument Lane. They included Vic Blumfield, who originated from Shrewsbury. In 1916 he and a friend went to the local sheds, where the GW and LNW operated side by side. The two friends tossed a coin to see who should apply to which company and Vic's outcome was a job with the LNW. He moved to Monument Lane in the early 1920s, progressing through the firing and driving links until, in 1955, he was ultimately able to call himself a Royal Train Driver. Vic used to chalk an image of a foaming pint of beer on the inside of the cab as a reminder to his fireman that he would be suitably rewarded at journey's end if he produced enough steam to satisfy Vic! Another man destined for the top link was 'Roger' (real name Ralph) Thornicroft, who originated from Rugby and whose father had been a driver in his home town.

Over the years there would often be numerous examples of long service at the shed and a ceremony held in January 1937 gives an insight into how a lengthy career was recognised at that time. Amongst those present were two Monument Lane drivers, H Jenkins and John Cornes, who had both given 47 years service, for which they received a Westminster chimes clock and pair of candlesticks.

THE SHED HIERARCHY FROM THE 1940s

By the time that World War II was underway the Shedmaster was Norman Sutherland Nicholas, who rose to the rank of Captain in the Royal Engineers during World War I. He came from Blackpool and later became a Major in the Home Guard. Known semi affectionately as 'Old Nick', he had trained as a draughtsman, and had a very good understanding of all things mechanical. Unfortunately, he was a man to whom the use of bad language came as second nature. That did not endear him to some of the female cleaners employed at the shed during World War II, as if they made a complaint to him about bad language they would receive a reply couched in similar terms.

Mr Nicholas was eventually promoted and transferred to Aston. He was succeeded at Monument Lane by Jack Little but Mr Nicholas later lost four toes in an accident at Bescot and that incident, although not fatal at the time, shortened his life, resulting in Jack Little being called to Aston.

The Running Shift Foreman was Harry Marshall, whose wife owned a guest house in the Edgbaston area of Birmingham; he later became Shedmaster at Bescot. He was followed by Tom Vickers, a former Crewe man who became Shedmaster himself at Monument Lane before moving on to Nuneaton and then returning to Crewe. After Tom Vickers' departure, Cumbrian Jack Lowe arrived from Tebay as Shedmaster. Ultimately Jack moved on to Stourbridge and then Saltley in similar posts.

A Running Foreman from the early 1950s was Arthur Warrington, a Burton on Trent man who returned to that town. Arthur Warrington was succeeded by Terry Smith, a premium apprentice who would later become became Shedmaster at Goole and then Stockport. His successor was John Dean, who took on the role of Running Foreman from 1952 to 1957. Also in that role was Bert Preston, a very experienced railwayman who was formerly a driver and Deputy Foreman at Bescot. He moved on to become a Locomotive Footplate

Inspector at New Street around 1960. The post was also covered by Sammy Plant. He originated from Bescot but had spent some time at Monument Lane as a driver before progressing to Foreman.

FITTERS AND SUPPORT STAFF

The Leading Fitter during the 1940s was Harry Austin. He was followed by Tom Vickers before his promotion to Shedmaster. The job of Leading Fitter fell to Frank Rigby after Tom Vickers' promotion. Frank, a former Ryecroft man, remained at Monument Lane for around fifteen years before taking up the position of Shedmaster at Bushbury in the late 1950s.

The fitters were Fred Ellison, Billy Myatt, Bob Norris – who stayed at work until the age of 71 – Harry Howard and Albert Pargetter. Another fitter, who was still at the shed in the 1950s, was Tommy Armitage, who always wore a white shirt, collar and tie and took it very badly if one of his workmates caused it to become stained in any way. By the 1950s Bob Inett and Tommy Attwood were fitters' mates who progressed to become fitters.

At the end of the 1930s the Boilersmith was Jack Slater. Supporting him were Tuber Walter Gibbons, Boiler Washers Arthur Featherstone and Charlie Lampitt, together with steam raisers Bob Burgham, Alf Lewis and Fred Oliver, who was a church verger at St John's Church, Ladywood. The shed labourers were Doug Stanley, Fred Taylor and Jack Brookes, who was formerly employed on the old coal stage. Jack Turner was employed on the ash pit and the Brickarch man was Len (Skid) Reeves.

In the Stores in 1940 were Billy Hughes, Tommy Freeth and Harry Davies. Billy Hughes progressed to Running Shift Foreman, whilst his colleagues became time clerks. Steam raisers were Alf Lewis, whose brother George, a fitter's mate, was killed in an accident at the shed in 1948, Fred Oliver and Frank Boulton.

One of the timekeepers and foreman's assistant, Jack Middleton, was a very skilled man with the paint brush and he was able to demonstrate his talents when preparing engines for railtour or Royal Train duty.

Tube Cleaners in the 1950s were Ronnie Saxon, Bert Parsons and Ernie (Spot) Harber, whilst the Boilersmith was a Geordie, Eric Dowie, who had been a shipyard boilersmith. 'Spot' Harber had been one of the few men who had been recruited as a 'temporary passed cleaner' to cover manpower shortages. Such men were not in the normal line of promotion and eventually came off the footplate to take on other shed duties.

In the 1950s the Chief Clerk was George Bailey, who retired in mid 1953. He was succeeded by Joe Stanley. The staff clerk was Billy Goodman and the clerical staff included two women, Mileage Clerk Miss Leighton and Stores Clerk Iris Kerr.

Bill Timmins, one of the shed's Ambulance Men, was the coaling plant operator. He was killed in an accident when working the plant on the day of the Harrow Rail accident, 8 October 1952.

Over at the diesel shed a newly created post of Mechanical Fitter fell to George Whittaker in 1956. Also at the diesel shed were Jack Evans, who had formerly worked for AEC on trucks, Bernard Brown, and Tom Harrison, who had joined the shed in 1954 as an apprentice. When the DMUs came the shifts embraced round the clock working and the men included Tommy Birchill, Albert Colley and Harry Ratley. The shed also had a contingent of female carriage cleaners known as 'Water Lilies'.

FOOTPLATE MEN

During World War II drivers were kept on beyond the age of 65. Three such men were Jimmy Slater, Jack Ball and Amos Goode, who were all in the banking link. In fact Amos Goode was still to be found on the footplate at the age of 71. Those men moved into the banking link to avoid the day to day rigours of the main line. A decade later that link included Tommy Hastings, Steve Reynolds, Ray Gower and Bert Carlill, who had been the driver on the last passenger train to Harborne in 1934. Another experienced driver at the shed around the time of World War II was Jack Allen, who became a well known Footplate Inspector in the area, passing out many men to become drivers.

Many Monument Lane men began their railway career away from Birmingham. Some came from very far afield, such as Bill Currie, who made the long journey from Beattock. Moor Row was a one-time base for Derek Tyson and in the 1950s five men could boast a knowledge of the Workington area. 'Spot' Harber began his days at Abergavenny, Sid Bounds had also worked in the Welsh valleys at Tredegar. Dick Bishop had worked over the Somerset and Dorset when based at Bath shed, and from the same part of the country came George Dixon, who began his career at Bristol Barrow Road.

From Llandudno Junction in North Wales came Les Jones. Les was nicknamed 'Cochyn' in his native Wales (anybody in Wales where Welsh was spoken was called Cochyn if they had red hair). He started as a cleaner at Llandudno Junction in 1942/43 and moved on loan to the Birmingham area when he was a passed cleaner. He decided to stay at Monument Lane and eventually rose to running shift foreman.

Men also transferred from local sheds to Monument Lane. From Aston came Frank Ward and amongst the men transferred in from Bescot were 'Doc' Neale, George Dance and Ronnie Ford, all of whom later returned to Bescot. Former Crewe men included Jack Williams Jack moved to Monument Lane from Crewe in 1937 together with three other firemen. Bushbury, Walsall and Coventry men also moved to the shed.

Some of the men has skills in other areas or devoted their time to serving the community. Frank Boston was a magician who entertained at children's parties. He also owned a newsagent's shop and used to bring in boxes of chocolates and cigarettes. Howard 'Ticker' Stanley was an accomplished watch repairer and William Albert Norman Jones was a Birmingham City Councillor.

The top link men included Ray Gower, who began his railway career at Bromsgrove around the time of World War I. Ray ended his working days on the New Street bank engines and he had rather unorthodox meal arrangements. For his drinks he brought a sterilised milk bottle, plugged with a piece of newspaper and into which the tea leaves and leftovers were poured at home during the previous day. For his lunch he kept an aluminium dish in which were a range of leftovers collected from the various meals; his enjoyment was topped off by a clay pipe. For all of his foibles he is fondly remembered. When walking to New Street another bank engine driver, Steve Reynolds, would stand in front of a statue of James Watt and berate him for his part in developing steam power.

There were always men with family connections at the shed. In later years they included brothers Len and Alan Carr, Phillip and Johnny Attwood, Albert and Fred Pargetter and Billy and Freddie Stephens. Freddie gained the Military Medal in World War II. George and Alf Lewis were also brothers, with George's son Reg becoming a top link driver at the shed. Phil and David Burford were also father and son and George and Sid Halfpenny had a similar relationship, as did Arthur Clowes and his son John. One other family connection is of interest. Reg Lewis, who was at the shed during World War II, believed that one of William Stanier's sons worked at the shed for a time.

Arthur Clowes, known as 'The Admiral', was a man beset by injuries and accidents but who fought his way back to work. At one time he was so severely burnt from a blowback that his chances of survival were seen as very low. However, not only did he recover, he also returned to the main line. With his wax moustache and a shirt that was always open – and a driving style frequently described as 'heavy handed' – 'The Admiral' is remembered by everyone from his era. One memory of him is when working the 5.27pm from Euston to Rugby with a Class '5'. On leaving Wolverton the 'Red Rose' passed, hauled by 46209 *Princess Beatrice*. By the time that Arthur reached Roade he had caught up with it!

In its last years the shed had a rapid turnover of Shedmasters, including Phillip Tudge and, finally, Colin Wood. Amongst the drivers when the shed closed were Jack Williams, Les Riddle, Les Holland and Brian Clarke, who ended his career as Depot Manager at New Street. Also present was Frank Ward, who finally retired as a driver with Virgin Trains. During his career Frank's driving experience ranged from Johnson 0-6-0s, some of which originated in the 1870s, to Inter City HSTs, introduced in the 1970s.

7

ANECDOTES AND INCIDENTS

ROLLS ROYCE LOCOMOTIVES

On one occasion Charles Macleur was working on a 'Claughton' which had arrived at the shed and he found a billy can full of tea, on a flat plate behind the cab steps. It transpired that it did not belong to any of the Monument Lane men. Instead, it had been left there by someone preparing the loco at Rugby shed. The billy can made the journey back with the next visiting Rugby crew. The comment was that the 'Claughtons' must have been very smooth runners.

A RUNAWAY NEAR CREWE

One day we took a 'Black 5' to Bescot to run a special fully loaded ballast train to Crewe. I can't remember the driver but I think he was a bit inexperienced and so was I with this sort of working. So off we set and went all the way to Whitmore Troughs. Then we started to run down to Crewe and as we got over the top it was going at a fine clip on the slow line and then when we came to braking the wheels locked on the engine and we were skidding down the slow line to Crewe with all this ballast behind us pushing like crazy.

Fortunately – and you might not believe this but it's true – we had a brake van right next to the tender and we had a brake van at the back with the guard in. We were going downhill, the wheels were skidding and we were just carrying on so I had to climb over the back of the tender and down onto the brake van next to the engine and put on the brakes in the brake van. That was enough to slow us down, otherwise we would never have slowed down enough to get into the siding. The engine got flats on its wheels by the way! (BS).

WINTER OF 1947

During the early part of 1947 all of the trains were late. I was in the Spare Link and I had to book on for the 5.15 to Lichfield that night. I got to the shed and we had a 'Jubilee'. Then Eric Reece came up to the carriage sidings with a 'Black 5' and hooked onto us. We were coupled together and we both went tender first- you couldn't turn at Lichfield. We were late going and we were first stop Gravelly Hill and then all stations. They stopped us at Sutton Coldfield and we were there for over half an hour. We were stopped at Sutton Coldfield because the snow had drifted up a bridge. Then we had to have a wrong line order for the trip back. We had a real job to get into Lichfield.

When we got to Lichfield there wasn't a water column, so we had to take water from a stand pipe. The Station Master and an Inspector were there and they told us that they would like us to try to get through the drift. They didn't know how long it would take so they rang the pub to provide drinks and sandwiches. There was a train to Burton at about 6pm from New Street with Burton men and a Midland 'Number 2' and they came through light engine – they left the coaches at Sutton. They took water and hooked onto us and they also sent a 'Super D' from Bescot with a plough and there were four engines – they shouldn't have done it because the bridges weren't made for that weight. When they set off we reached Sutton and the 'D' and the '2' came off. They managed to get a tank engine from Aston to put the Burton train into the sidings. We didn't get to New Street until 2 o'clock – mind we had some lovely cheese and cress sandwiches from the pub.

Incidentally, at that time they had to leave the Soho Pool engine there for about a week – they couldn't get it out. They had to throw out the fire. (GD).

THE BIG FREEZE OF 1963

During the Big Freeze of 1962/63, which caused great hardship across the country, one parcels working illustrated the extent to which railwaymen were affected. On Wednesday 23 January Derek Tyson and Frank Ward worked the 10.40pm parcels to Euston. The train left New Street at about 11.00pm with Class '5' 45131 and they were not destined to be relieved until 2pm the following day, by which time they had reached Bletchley, still short of their destination. They eventually came back passenger after 21 hours on duty.

'THE ADMIRAL' AT WORK

The Glasgow sleepers arrived in New Street behind a brand new 'Britannia' and derailed at the trap points. The train was duly shunted back from the derailed loco into another platform and urgent requests were made to us to ask if we could work the sleepers forward. The Admiral was in the office at the time and on hearing this he volunteered to work it to Crewe, even though he had already come from London. He took 44942, which had not been disposed of or prepared, straight down to New Street. Shortly afterwards there was a roar as 44942 came through the tunnel at full blast with 16 on and a marvellous firework display. The Admiral must have woken half of Brum that night! (TS).

DISRUPTION TO THE RUSH HOUR

An extremely disruptive incident occurred on 23 July 1953 when Class '5' 44942 was derailed at the shed, preventing movement of engines off the site. That led to the cancellation of three key rush hour services on the Lichfield line. Eventually the 6.02pm for Burton via Lichfield departed, with a Burton 4-4-0 hauling a train that was somewhat overloaded!

RUNAWAYS ON THE HARBORNE BRANCH

A major occurrence took place on Saturday 31 October 1953, happily without loss of life, when ten loaded coal wagons slipped away on the downward gradient of the Harborne line. The trucks derailed at Harborne Junction on the Wolverhampton to Birmingham line, crashing into the canal and causing a blockage on the main line.

A similar incident had occurred in 1905, although with less disruption on the main line.

DIESEL INCIDENTS

There were no serious incidents involving loss of life in the diesel days, although on 19 December 1956 during dense fog one of the Monument Lane Units crashed into a light engine near Proof House Junction on the approaches to New Street. Driver Dick Bishop was badly injured and hospitalised for some time. The unit involved was M79643/M79122 and M79643 was badly damaged, although it was repaired.

A potentially serious incident occurred in the diesel shed yard when three goods wagons were derailed and ran into a stationery diesel shunter. One of the wagons was a tanker containing 3,000 gallons a fuel but it did not ignite. Shunter Albert Colley was in the vicinity of the accident but he fortunately escaped injury.

A FINAL MEMORY

The last years of the shed were difficult times with manpower shortages and limited investment in maintaining the declining fleet of steam locomotives. However, across the rail network there were many men with the dedication and skills to overcome the adversities and Monument Lane was no exception. Let Brian Clarke have the final word.

One day as a fireman back in 1959 we used to lodge at Camden on a Friday night, book on the next day on the Saturday and we used to work the 4.35pm from Euston to Wolverhampton. On this day in particular we had 45647 Sturdee, *a Bushbury engine. Just as we were about to come off the shed a Bushbury fireman said to me, "God help you with that thing – she's been booked 'not steaming'".*

We went down into Euston and hooked onto the train – we'd got a full train with about 12 or 13 on and away we came. When we stopped at Watford we'd had no problems with her, and away out of Watford, then stop at Northampton – still no problems. Leaving Northampton is quite a climb up to Long Buckby and my mate Roger Thornicroft was working the engine quite hard, as he had to do, so I'm feeding the engine little and often – sixes and eights. Then, coming up the bank the safety valves lifted – that was against the injector, against being worked hard and with an engine that was booked 'not steaming'. That day I really got job satisfaction (BC).

APPENDIX 1: MONUMENT LANE
LOCOMOTIVE ALLOCATIONS

1912	5 January 1935	1 January 1940
'Experiment'	LMS Compound 4-4-0	LMS Compound 4-4-0
507 *Sarmatian*, 1455	1113, 1157, 1166, 1167,	1122, 1166, 1169
Herefordshire	1168, 1169, 1172, 1173	
'Precursor'	MR '1F' 0-6-0T	MR '1F' 0-6-0T
184 *Havelock* 1312 *Ionic*	1777, 1818	1726
6ft 6in 'Jumbo'	LNW '1P' 2-4-2T	Stanier Class '4' 2-6-4T
1519 *Duchess*	6671, 6748	2449, 2450, 2451, 2487,
		2567, 2579
5ft 6in 'Jumbo'	LNW '2P' 4-4-2T	MR '3F' 0-6-0
742 *Spitfire*	6821, 6822	3915
'Superheater Tank'	LNW '1P' 0-6-2T	Stanier '5MT' 4-6-0
632, 1692, 1728, 1734	6894, 6900, 6923, 6924,	5395
	6925, 6926, 6927	
'18in Tank'	LNW '3P' 4-6-2T	LNW '1P' 0-6-2T
16, 280, 345, 495,	6950, 6956, 6957, 6994	6876, 6878, 6883, 6923,
593, 1563, 1588		6925, 6927, 6935
'5ft 6in Tank'	MR '3F' 0-6-0T	MR '3F' 0-6-0T
910, 2148	1953	1953
'4ft 6in Tank'	LMS '3F' 0-6-0T	LMS '3F' 0-6-0T
765, 769, 2245	16450, 16451	16465
'19in Goods'	LNW 'G1'/ 'G2a'	MR '2F' 0-6-0
1302, 1461, 2270	9042	22904, 22913, 22920,
		22928, 23005, 23006,
		23007, 3503

CONTINUED

1912	5 January 1935	1 January 1940
'18 in Goods'	LNW 'George V'	LNW Special '2F' 0-6-0T
128, 1265	5338 *Thomas Houghton*	27351, 27353
'DX'	LNW 'Prince of Wales'	LNW '2F' 0-6-2T
3029	25706 *Canning*	27664, 7742
'C'	MR '2F' 0-6-0	
2534	22918, 22928, 23005,	
	23006, 23007	
'17in Coal'	LNW '2F' 0-6-2T	
750, 778, 2046	27594, 7742	
'Coal Tank'		
220, 1063, 1203,		
1254, 2461		
'Square ST'		
12, 2439		
'Special Tank'		
757, 924, 1123, 1355,		
3364		
'4ft Shunter'		
3244		

1 January 1948	1 January 1955	1 August 1960
LMS Compound 4-4-0	Stanier '3P' 2-6-2T	Stanier '3P' 2-6-2T
1111, 1116, 1153,	40108, 40118	40108, 40129
1154, 1172		
Fairburn Class '4' 2-6-4T	LMS Compound 4-4-0	LMS Compound 4-4-0
2262, 2263, 2264,	40933, 40936, 41090	40936, 41168
2265, 2267		
Stanier Class '4' 2-6-4T	Fairburn Class '4' 2-6-4T	Fairburn '4P' 2-6-4T
2450, 2451, 2482,	42267, 42674	42267
2488, 2489, 2579,		
2659		
LMS '4F' 0-6-0	Fowler Class '4' 2-6-4T	Stanier '4P' 2-6-4T
4057, 4514, 4592	42419, 42420, 42421,	42488
	42422	

CONTINUED

1 January 1948	1 January 1955	1 August 1960
Stanier '5MT' 4-6-0 5495	Stanier Class '4' 2-6-4T 42579	LMS '4F' 0-6-0 44057, 44444, 44490, 44514
LNW '1P' 0-6-2T 6876, 6878, 6922	MR '3F' 0-6-0 43231	Stanier '5MT' 4-6-0 44842, 45034, 45071, 45111, 45134, 45188, 45301, 45308
MR '2F' 0-6-0 58117, 58124, 58177, 58178, 58179, 58273	LMS '4F' 0-6-0 44057, 44361, 44490, 44506, 44512, 44514, 44592	LMS '3F' 0-6-0T 47474, 47494, 47561
LNW 'Cauliflower' 0-6-0 58429	Stanier '5MT' 4-6-0 44942, 45051, 45390	MR '2F' 0-6-0 58135, 58185, 58220, 58271
LNW '2F' 0-6-2T 58916	MR '2F' 0-6-0 58117, 58124, 58178, 58179, 58185, 58286	

Locomotive allocations courtesy of the London and North Western Railway Society and Richard Strange's 'Steam Archive Services'.

APPENDIX 2: MONUMENT LANE SAMPLE DUTIES 1B LINK 1956 AND 1A LINK 1957

1B LINK 1956

	Sun	Mon	Tues	Wed	Thurs	Fri	Sat
1 Jan 1956	Off duty	5/00 New St - Lichfield 42267(3E)	5/00 New St - Lichfield 42267(3E)	5/00 New St - Lichfield 42267(3E)	5/00 New St - Lichfield 42267(3E)	5/00 New St - Lichfield 42267(3E)	1/10 New St - Wolv W737 44716(2A)
8 Jan 1956	Off duty	5.15 New St - Wolv (Parcels) 45709(3B)	12.20 New St - Rugby (Parcels) 45437(2A)	12.20 New St - Rugby (Parcels) 45437(2A)	12.20 New St - Rugby (Parcels) 44909(2A)	12.20 New St - Rugby (Parcels) 45050(2A)	12.20 New St - Rugby (Parcels) 45403(2A)
15 Jan 1956	6.50 New St - Rugby 41165(2A)	7.50 New St - Burton 42420(3E)	7.50 New St - Burton 42421(3E)	7.50 New St - Burton 44506(3E)	7.50 New St - Burton 42419(3E)	7.50 New St - Burton 42419(3E)	7.50 New St - Burton 42419(3E)
22 Jan 1956	Off duty	3/55 New St - Rugby 44833(2A)	3/55 New St - Rugby 44833(2A)	3/55 New St - Rugby 44833(2A)	3/55 New St - Rugby 44833(2A)	12/30 New St - Euston 44833(2A)	3/40 Oldbury 41090(3E)
29 Jan 1956	Off duty	9.20 New St - Liverpool 46137(5A) 3/00 Liverpool - Crewe 44897(3D)	5.40 Crewe - New St 45493(2A)	9.20 New St - Liverpool 46155(5A) 3/00 Liverpool - Crewe 45397(3D)	5.40 Crewe - New St 46137(2A)	9.20 New St - Liverpool 46161(9A) 3/00 Liverpool - Crewe 44897(3D)	5.40 Crewe - New St 44909 (2A)

CONTINUED

	Sun	Mon	Tues	Wed	Thurs	Fri	Sat
5 Feb 1956		4/48 New St - Lichfield 40125(3B)	4/48 New St - Lichfield 40125(3B)	4/48 New St - Lichfield 40125(3B)	4/48 New St - Lichfield 40125(3B)	4/48 New St - Lichfield 40125(3B)	7/40 New St - Northampton 45548(5A)
12 Feb 1956	Off duty	2.50 New St - Leamington 46118(5A) 7.55 Leamington - New St 46118(5A)	2.50 New St - Leamington 46150(5A) 7.55 Leamington - New St 46150(5A)	2.50 New St - Leamington 46118(5A) 7.55 Leamington - New St 46118(5A)	2.50 New St - Leamington 46110(5A) 7.55 Leamington - New St 46110(5A)	2.50 New St - Leamington 46129(5A) 7.55 Leamington - New St 46129(5A)	2.50 New St - Leamington 45591(5A) 7.55 Leamington - New St 45591(5A)
19 Feb 1956	Off duty	Off duty	10/40 New St - Euston (Parcels) 45741(3B)	5/20 Euston - Rugby 45429(1A) 7/00 Euston - New St (relieve at Rugby) 46155(5A)	10/40 New St - Euston (Parcels) 45552(3B)	5/20 Euston - Rugby 45372(1A) 7/00 Euston - New St (relieve at Rugby) 46118(5A)	

1A LINK 1957

	Sun	Mon	Tues	Wed	Thurs	Fri	Sat
30 Dec 1956	11/0 New St bank 40108(3E)	Off duty	7.10 New St - Manchester 44750(9A)	12.05 Crewe - New St 44941(9A) Relieve New St Bank 40108(3E)	7.10 New St - Manchester 44750(9A)	12.05 Crewe - New St 44741(9A) Relieve New St Bank 40108(3E)	7.10 New St - Manchester
6 Jan 1957	12.45 Crewe - New St 44938(9A)	12/10 New St - Manchester 44759(5A)	12/10 New St - Manchester 45302(5A)	12/10 New St - Manchester 45131(5B)	12/10 New St - Manchester 45703(5A)	12/10 New St - Manchester 44761(5A)	2/20 Euston - New St (Assist) 44897(3D)

CONTINUED

	Sun	Mon	Tues	Wed	Thurs	Fri	Sat
		4/30 Manchester - New St 44759(5A)	4/30 Manchester - New St 45302(5A)	4/30 Manchester - New St 45131(5B)	4/30 Manchester - New St 45703(5A)	4/30 Manchester - New St 44761(5A)	
13 Jan 1957	Off duty	7.10 New St - Manchester 45670(8A)	12.05 Crewe - New St 44752(9A) Relieve New St Bank 42579(3E)	7.10 New St - Manchester 44938(9A)	12.05 Crewe - New St 45540(9A) Relieve New St Bank 42579(3E)	7.10 New St - Manchester 44741(9A)	12.05 Crewe - New St 45595(9A) Relieve New St Bank 42579(3E)
20 Jan 1957	9.35 New St - Stafford 44752(9A)	5/0 New St - Rugby 45308(3E)	5/0 New St - Rugby 45034(3E)	5/0 New St - Rugby 44749(9A)	5/0 New St - Rugby 45114(3D)	5/0 New St - Rugby 45287(3B)	1/0 Monument Lane Carriage shed 44514(3E)
27 Jan 1957	Relieve W705 45652(9A)	12/45 Spon Lane 43231(3E)	12/45 Spon Lane 43231(3E)	12/45 Spon Lane 58306(3E)	12/45 Spon Lane 43231(3E)	12/45 Spon Lane 43187(3E)	1/0 Monument Lane Carriage shed 44514(3E)
3 Feb 1957	Off duty	5/40 Oldbury 44490(3E)	3.0 Oldbury 44490(3E)	3.0 Oldbury 44057(3E)	3.0 Oldbury 44057(3E)	3.0 Oldbury 44057(3E)	3.0 Oldbury 44057(3E)
10 Feb 1957	Off duty	6/25 New St - Stafford 42814(9A)	10/40 New St - Euston (Parcels) 10000(1A)	5/20 Euston - Rugby 45381(1A)	10/40 New St - Euston (Parcels) 10000(1A)	5/20 Euston - Rugby 45025(1A)	7/40 New St - Northampton 45545(5A)
17 Feb 1957	Off duty	5.56 New St - Stoke 42552(3E)	5.56 New St - Stoke 42552(3E)	5.56 New St - Stoke 42552(3E)	Off duty	5.56 New St - Stoke 42552(3E)	5.56 New St - Stoke 42552(3E)

CONTINUED

	Sun	Mon	Tues	Wed	Thurs	Fri	Sat
24 Feb 1957	4/30 New St - Euston 46100(1B)	10/40 New St - Euston (Parcels) 45439(3B)	5/20 Euston - Rugby 45278(1A)	10/40 New St - Euston (Parcels) 45015(1A)	5/20 Euston - Rugby 45430(1A)	10/40 New St - Euston (Parcels) 45742(3B)	4/37 Euston - New St 45709(3B)
3 Mar 1957	Off duty	7/0 Stechford 45519(9A)	8.30 New St - Euston (Assist) 45686(3B)	8.30 New St - Euston (Assist) 45257(3E)	8.30 New St - Euston (Assist) 45257(3E)	8.30 New St - Euston (Assist) 45257(3E)	7.15 New St - Euston W714 45257(3E)
10 Mar 1957	Off duty	Off duty	12.2 New St - Stafford 44687(9A)	12.2 New St - Stafford 44748(9A)	12.2 New St - Stafford 44840(9A)	12.2 New St - Stafford 44686(9A)	12.2 New St - Stafford 44750(9A)
17 Mar 1957	6.0 Soho Ballast 44490(3E)	3/53 New St - Rugby 44915(2A)	3/53 New St - Rugby 44870(2A)	3/53 New St - Rugby 44909(2A)	3/53 New St - Rugby 44833(2A)	3/53 New St - Rugby 44833(2A)	12/10 New St - Manchester 45109(9A)

Railway terminology of the period has been used where 12.00 is am and 12/00 denotes pm. Shed Codes: 1A Willesden, 1B Camden, 2A Rugby, 3B Bushbury, 3D Aston, 3E Monument Lane, 5A Crewe North, 5B Crewe South, 8A Edge Hill (Liverpool), 9A Longsight (Manchester). Information courtesy of Frank Ward.

APPENDIX 3: DRIVERS BY LINK IN 1951

1A Link Drivers	1B Link Drivers	No 2 Link	No 3 Link
Teddy Lamb	Wally Beech	George Timms	Ernie Link
Roger Thornicroft	Dick Challenor	Billy Higgins	Dennis Cheetham
Fred Hulse	Bob Jones *'Capt Bob'*	Albert Jepson	George Phillips
Billy Collis	Billy Cornes	George Adams	Phil Burford
Ray Gower	Dennis Reece	Joe Hayes	Ronnie Tongue
George Middleton	Jack Moylan	Frank Boston	Sid Halfpenny
Vic Blumfield	Harold Little	Eric Asbury	Harold Fletcher
Harold Taylor	Cyril *'Dixie'* Dean	George Keats	Fred *'Spud'* Murphy
Bert Bissell	George Williams	Bob Jones *'Blonde Bob'*	Sammy Plant
Charlie Sandells	Arthur Clowes *'The Admiral'*	Jackie Lee	Billy *'Tallipot Bill'* Beech
Freddie Stephens	Dick Lloyd	Harry Carrick	Sid Cooper
Harry Milward	Harold Onions	Len Leavesley	Arthur Baglin
Spare Link	**Shunting Link**	**Disposal Link**	**Tipton Drivers**
Jack Williams	Frank Boardman	Albert *'Sailor Jack'* Slater	Len Neville
H 'Taffy' Hughes	Arthur Dawborn	Bert Taylor	Billy Emerson
Cliff Jones	Alf *'Boy Scout'* Paddock	Frank Sumner	
Doug Piggin	Arthur Paddock	Howard Stanley	
Ernie Jones	Martin Grogan		
Ken Green	Billy Bradshaw		
	Joe Simmons		
	Billy Preston		

CONTINUED

New St Bank Link	Shunting Link	Passed Fireman	Tipton Fireman
Bert Carlill	Jack Johnson	Harold Orme	Alan Parker
Tommy Turner	Tommy Dodd	Ernie Rowe	
Tommy Hastings	Wally Welstead	Dick Bishop	
Steve Reynolds	Ernie 'Winky Pop' Jones	Reg Lewis	
		Tommy Wilkes	
		Fred Massey	
		Cliff Wall	
		George Milward	
		Vic Perks	
		Jack Scrivens	
		Bernard Davies	
		Derek Tyson	

New St South End Link			Albion Drivers
Arthur 'Curly' Turner			Billy Disley
Billy Bevan			Arthur Rawson
Tommy Evans			
			Albion Fireman
			Sam Adams

APPENDIX 4: MONUMENT LANE LOCOMOTIVE WORKINGS SUMMER 1955

MONDAY TO FRIDAY

Train Time	Train	Class of Engine	Loco Turn	Men's Turn	Remarks
12.2	New St - Stafford (Parcels)	2-6-0 5MT	9A/33	150	Reman 5/8 Napton on shed
12.20	New Street - Rugby (Parcels)	5MT	2A/1	120	Off 5/39 x Rugby
2.50	New Street to Leamington (Parcels)	7P	5A/30	133	On Monday, loco is off 3/42pm from Crewe (Sun) Tuesday to Friday loco is off 7/0pm Euston - New Street
3.0	Oldbury Yard	4F	215	215	Trip 207. Mondays Excepted
4.0	Mon Lane Yard	Mid 2F	237	237	Target 33. Mondays Excepted
4.0	Soho Yard	3F	255	255	Trip 36. Mondays Excepted
4.13	New St - Walsall (Newspapers)	Class 4 tank	50	50	On return is remanned on shed for 12/25 New St - Lichfield
4.35	Four Oaks	4F	33	33	Trip 155
5.0	Monument Lane	Mid 2F	235	235	Target 33
5.0	M&B	Mid 2F	270	270	Trip 193
5.15	New St - Wolverhampton (Parcels)	6P	3B/6	160	Mondays Only. Off 5.15 Wolves (Saturdays Only)
5.30	Tipton Yard	Mid 2F	294	294	Trip 206. Departs 5.40 on Mondays
5.40	Oldbury Yard	4F	215	215	Trip 207. Mondays Only

CONTINUED

Train Time	Train	Class of Engine	Loco Turn	Men's Turn	Remarks
5.50	Soho Yard	3F	255	255	Trip 36
5.55	New St - Stafford	Class 4 tank	5C/1	151	On Mondays, loco is off 5/25 x Coventry (Sun)
		6P	8A/13	151	Tuesdays to Fridays is off 9/35 Stafford - New Street (Parcels)
5.56	New St - Stoke	Class 4 tank	64	64	
6.0	New Street North End Bank	Class 3 tank	80	80	Mondays only
6.0	New Street South End Pilot	Class 3 tank	90	90	Mondays only
6.12	Soho Tip	4F	29	29	Trip 207A
6.22	New Street to Lichfield	Class 4 tank	68	68	Loco returns to act as Carriage Shed shunt engine. Remanned at Carr Shed for 5/0pm Mon Lane to Lichfield
6.30	Carr Shed & 12.10pm New St - Manchester	5MT	2	171	
6.39	Spon Lane	3F	225	225	Trip 208
7.10	New St - Manchester	5MT	5A/86	104	Mondays loco is off 12/10 from Manchester (Sun)
			84G/37	104	Tuesdays to Fridays is off 12.05 parcels from Crewe
7.22	Motor	Class 2 tank	96	96	
7.34	New Street - Coventry	Class 4 tank	9A/39	136	Off 10/10 x Stafford SAT
7.37	New Street - Rugeley	Class 4 tank	56	56	
7.50	New Street - Burton	Class 4 tank	38	38	Remanned in New St for 12/48 Coventry
8.04	Soho Pool	4F	200	200	Trip 185
8.33	Motor	Class 2 tank	98	98	

CONTINUED

Train Time	Train	Class of Engine	Loco Turn	Men's Turn	Remarks
8.45	New Street - Peterborough	5MT	2A/3	121	On Mondays loco is off 8/55 x Euston (Sun) Tuesday - Friday reman 3.19am from Rugby on shed
9.40	Albion	Mid 2F	285	285	Trip 198
12/25	New Street - Lichfield	Class 4 tank	51	51	Reman 4.13 Walsall on shed. Later remanned in New St for 7/4 Coventry
12/30	New Street - Euston	Compound	7	110	Fridays only. Coupled. Returns assisting 5/50 from Euston
12/48	New Street - Coventry	Class 4 tank	39	138	Reman 7.50 from New Street to Burton in New St on its return
2/20	New Street - Euston	5MT	5D/301	115	Fridays only. Reman 1/22 from Brindley Heath in New St
2/30	New Street - Euston	Compound	8	111	Fridays only. Coupled. Returns assisting 6/55 from Euston
2/50	New St - Rugby	Class 4 tank	2A/38	123	Reman 10.52 from Rugby on shed Peterborough
3/55	New St - Peterboro	5MT	2A/5	125	Off 10.25 x Peterborough
3/58	New St - Coventry	Class 4 tank	66	66	Off 5.56 Stoke
4/0	Carr Shed	4F	26	26	Remanned at Mon Lane for 7/32 freight to Bushbury
4/30	New St - Euston	Comp 4P	9	117	Fridays only. Assisting. Returns coupled to 9/35 from Euston
4/48	New St - Lichfield	Class 3 tank	3B/11	163	Off 1/22 x Coventry
5/0	New St - Euston	5MT	2A/7	2A/272	Off 5.40 x Crewe SAT
5/8	New St - Napton	2-6-0 5MT	9A/33	135	Off 5.35 Parcels x Stafford SAT. Tuesday - Friday off 3.35 Parcels x Stafford
5/23	New St - Rugby	5MT	2A/14	126	Off 1/52 x Coventry
5/27	New St - Lichfield	4F	34	34	Off 4.35 Four Oaks

CONTINUED

Train Time	Train	Class of Engine	Loco Turn	Men's Turn	Remarks
5/42	Four Oaks	4F	30	30	Off 6.12 Soho Tip
6/12	New St - Rugeley	Class 4 tank	5C/3	3C/99	Off 6.5 x Rugeley
6/30	New St - Rugby	5MT	2A/3	2A/278	2A Engine & Men off 3/17 x Rugby (8.45 Peterborough engine)
7/40	New St - Euston	5MT	2A/14	138	Off 2/20 x Rugby
9/40	New St - Rugby	5MT	2A/1	2A/68	Reman 4/3 x Bletchley
10/40	New St - Euston	6P	3B/1	101	Off 5/57 x Wolverhampton
11/40	LE to Marton Jct	4F	17B/607	17B/673	Off 12/20 x Bushbury

SATURDAY

Train Time	Train	Class of Engine	Loco Turn	Men's Turn	Remarks
12.2	New St - Stafford	2-6-0 5MT	9A/33	150	Reman 8/45 x Leamington on shed
12.20	New St - Rugby	5MT	2A/1	2A/288	Off 5/39 x Rugby FRI
1.30	Mon Lane	Mid 2F	239	239	Target 33
2.50	New St - Leamington	Comp 4P	7	134	Returns 1/55 x Leamington (off 12/30 FRI)
3.0	Oldbury	4F	215	215	Trip 207
4.0	Soho	3F	255	255	Trip 36
4.13	New St - Walsall + 12.10 New St - Manchester	5MT	2	171	
5.15	New St - Wolverhampton	6P	3B/6	161	Off 3/0 x Euston FRI
5.40	Tipton	Mid 2F	297	297	Trip 206
5.56	New St - Stoke	Class 4 tank	64	64	
6.2	Soho Tip	4F	29	29	Trip 207A
6.10	M&B	2F	272	272	Trip 193
6.21	Spon Lane	3F	226	226	Trip 208
6.22	New St - Lichfield	Class 4 tank	70	70	

CONTINUED

Train Time	Train	Class of Engine	Loco Turn	Men's Turn	Remarks
6.25	Stechford	4F	35	35	Trip 155
6.27	Albion	2F	286	286	Trip 198
7.0	New St - Manchester	5MT	84G/37	105	Off 12.5 parcels x Crewe
7.17	New St - Euston	6P	1B/52	112	Off 6/55 asst x Euston FRI 17 June. Then from 24 June off 6/45 x Euston FRI
7.22	Motor	Class 2 tank	96	96	
7.34	New St - Leamington	Class 4 tank	3B/12	140	Off 11/00 x Bushbury Freight
7.37	New St - Rugeley	Class 4 tank	57	57	
7.50	New St - Burton	Class 4 tank	40	40	
8.04	Soho Pool	4F	202	202	Trip 185
8.05	New St - Ely	5MT	3	141	Returns 2/7 x Ely
8.10	New St - Crewe		2A/13	145	Reman 6.42 x Rugby in New St
8.18	New St - Euston		3B/2	113	Reman 7/52 x Walsall in New St
8.33	Motor	Class 2 tank	98	98	
8.35	New St - Crewe	5MT	10C/13	146	Off 4.20 Ship Canal - Bushbury Freight FRI
8.45	New St - Peterborough	5MT	2A/3	2A/265	2A Engine & Men off 3.25 x Rugby
9.0	New St - Blackpool	Comp 4P	8	144	
9.20	New St - Crewe	5MT	4	147	Returns 1/18 x Crewe
10.5	New St - Euston	6P	21	110	Off 4/25 x Euston FRI
11.40	New St - Mitre Bridge	5MT	3C/4	116	Reman 11.5 x Walsall
11.53	New St - Four Oaks	Class 4 tank	53	53	
1/28	New St - Crewe		9A/57	148	Reman 10.45 x Hastings in New St

CONTINUED

Train Time	Train	Class of Engine	Loco Turn	Men's Turn	Remarks
2/50	New St - Rugby	Class 4 tank	3C/38	124	Off 6.52 x Brownhills
3/55	New St - Peterborough	5MT	2A/1	2E/63	2A Engine & Men off 12/23 x Northampton
3/58	New St - Coventry	Class 4 tank	58	58	Reman 7.37 Rugeley on shed
4/6	New St - Walsall	5MT	9	164	Reman 10.45 x Hastings in New St
4/22	New St - Lichfield	Class 4 tank	71	71	Off 6.22 Lichfield
4/29	New St - Walsall		5B/2?	159	Reman 2/10 x Euston in New St
5/10	Bushbury	4F	36	3B/327	Off 6.25 Stechford
5/23	New St - Rugby	Comp 4P	2A/40	2A/274	Off 11.2 x Rugby
5/50	New St - Coventry	Class 4 tank	61	61	Off 5.56 Stoke
6/13	New St - Rugeley	4F	48	48	
6/30	New St - Rugby	5MT	2A/3	2A/275	2A Engine & Men off 3/39 x Coventry
7/40	New St - Euston	6P	5A/25	126	Off 2/20 x Rugby
10/47	New St - Rugeley	Class 4 tank	3C/39	3C/39	Off 2/50 Rugby

SUNDAY

Train Time	Train	Class of Engine	Loco Turn	Men's Turn	Remarks
3.10	Dudley	Class 4 tank	60	60	Remanned in New St for banking
6.50	New St - Rugby	5MT	2A/5	129	12/7 x Rugby
7.50	Soho	2F	260	260	Trip 40
8.0	Carr Shed	Class 4 tank	72	72	
9.35	New St - Stafford	6P/5F	9A/12	153	Off 12.45 x Crewe
10.40	New St - Coventry	Class 4 tank			Reman 7.42 x Stoke in New St
2/40	New St - Leamington	Class 4 tank	54	54	

CONTINUED

Train Time	Train	Class of Engine	Loco Turn	Men's Turn	Remarks
4/30	New St - Euston	6P/5F	1B/42	114	
7/25	New St - Rugby	Comp 4P	2A/35	128	Off 7.26 x Rugby
11/0	Bank	Class 3 tank	88	88	

Additional shed codes to those in Appendix 2: 2E Northampton, 3C Walsall, 5C Stafford, 5D Stoke, 10C Patricroft, 17B Burton, 84G Shrewsbury. Information courtesy of John Dean.

APPENDIX 5: MONUMENT LANE
LOCAL TRIP AND SHUNTING WORKINGS
1883 AND 1938

TABLE 1 – 1883

Location	Arrive	Depart
Monument Lane mpd		6.12am
Soho	6.15am	6.55am
Smethwick Jct	7.00am	7.30am
Spon Lane	7.25am	8.30am
Spon Lane Basin	8.35am (breakfast 30 mins)	12.15pm
Dudley Port	Water	
Albion	12.35pm (dinner 30 mins)	5.05pm
Oldbury		6.15pm
Spon Lane	6.20pm	6.30pm
Soho		6.55pm
Monument Lane mpd	7.05pm	

TABLE 2 – 1938

No.10 – SPON LANE AND SPON LANE BASIN SHUNTING ENGINE (SUSPENDED)

	Arr	Dep		Arr	Dep
Mon Lane Shed		8.12am LE	Dudley Port	9.45pm (SX)	12.50am LE (MSX)
Spon Lane	8.30am	1.55pm LE	Mon Lane Shed	1.10am (MSX)	
Tipton	2.9pm	4.0pm LE	Bloomfield	6.0pm	8.40pm LE (SO)
Dudley Port	4.3pm	5.55pm LE	Dudley Port	8.45pm SO	1.15am LE (Sun)
Bloomfield Jct	6.0pm	9.40pm LE (SX)	Mon Lane Shed	1.35am (Sun)	

No.36 – SOHO SHUNTING ENGINE – CLASS 2 FREIGHT ENGINE

	Arr	Dep		Arr	Dep
Mon Lane Shed		4.8am (MO) LE	Soho	4.12am (MO) shunt	11.50pm LE (SX)
Mon Lane Shed		2.0am (MX) LE	Soho	2.8am (MX) shunt	2.50am (Sun)
			Mon Lane Shed	11.55pm (SX)	
			Oldbury	3.0am	3.45am (Sun)
			Mon Lane Shed	4.0am (Sun)	

No.40 – SOHO NEW SIDINGS SHUNTING ENGINE – CLASS 2 FREIGHT ENGINE

	Arr	Dep		Arr	Dep
Mon Lane Shed		8.54am LE	Mon Lane Shed	4.4pm	
Soho New Sidings	9.0am shunt	3.55pm LE			

No.181 – MONUMENT LANE AND HARBORNE TRIP ENGINE – CLASS 1 TANK ENGINE

	Arr	Dep (SX)		Arr	Dep (SO)
New Street	–	–			12.40pm
Mon Lane		4.48pm LE	Mon Lane	–	–
Harborne	5.2pm	7.15pm	Harborne	12.58pm	3.32pm
Monument Lane Goods	7.35pm	LE to New St	Monument Lane	3.57pm	Coal and LE to New St

No.185 – SOHO POOL SHUNTING ENGINE – CLASS 2 FREIGHT ENGINE
UNTIL 15 OCTOBER 1938 INCLUSIVE (SX)

	Arr	Dep		Arr	Dep
Mon Lane Shed	–	10.20am LE	Bescot		12.30am (MX)
Soho Pool	10.34am	8.0pm (shunt)	Soho Pool	1.16am (MX)	1.57am (MX) LE
Bescot	8.27pm	10.0pm	Mon Lane	2.24am (MX)	
Soho Pool	10.31pm	11.25pm			
Bescot	11.57pm				

No.185 – SOHO POOL SHUNTING ENGINE – CLASS 2 FREIGHT ENGINE
COMMENCING 17 OCTOBER 1938 (SX)

| | SATURDAYS EXCEPTED | | | SATURDAYS ONLY | |
	Arr	Dep		Arr	Dep
Mon Lane Shed	–	10.20am LE	Mon Lane Shed	–	10.20am LE
Soho Pool	10.34am	10.0pm LE	Soho Pool	10.34am	8.8pm
Mon Lane Shed	10.19pm		Bescot	8.35pm	10.0pm
			Soho Pool	10.31pm	11.0pm LE
			Aston Goods	11.16pm	11.30pm
			Mon Lane	12.2am (Sun)	

No.185A – SOHO POOL SHUNTING ENGINE – CLASS 2 FREIGHT ENGINE
COMMENCING 17 OCTOBER 1938

	Arr	Dep		Arr	Dep
Mon Lane Shed	–	7.15pm (SX)	Bescot	11.57am	12.30am
Soho Pool	7.29pm	8.8pm (SX)	Soho Pool LE	1.16am	1.57am LE
Bescot	8.35pm	10.0pm	Mon Lane Shed	2.24am	
Soho Pool	10.31pm	11.25am			

No.193 – MONUMENT LANE AND HARBORNE TRIP ENGINE – CLASS 2
TANK ENGINE

	Arr	Dep		Arr	Dep
Monument Lane		7.28am	Harborne	7.46am	8.42am
			Monument Lane	8.55am LE to shed	

No.194 – MONUMENT LANE AND HARBORNE TRIP ENGINE – CLASS 2
TANK ENGINE

	Arr	Dep		Arr	Dep
New Street		8.22am ES	Harborne	10.20am	11.5am
Monument Lane	8.27am	9.2am	Monument Lane	11.24 LE to shed	
Hagley Road	9.17am	10.15am			

No.198 – ALBION AND MONUMENT LANE ENGINE – CLASS 2 FREIGHT ENGINE

	Arr	Dep		Arr	Dep
Mon Lane Shed		4.20am (MO) LE	Oldbury	2.0pm*	2.55pm E&B (MX)
Albion	4.39am (MO)	6.10am LE MX Train MO	Spon Lane Basin	2.58pm*	3.30pm
Oldbury	6.15am	7.15am LE	Oldbury	3.33pm	3.50pm (MX) E&B
Albion	7.20am*	1.55pm	Albion	3.55pm	–
Oldbury			Albion		7.13pm (SO) LE
			Mon Lane Shed	7.33pm	

*shunt

E&B – engine and brake van

The engine to make trips to Albion Gas Works Siding as required. The first trip to leave at 11.30am

As can be seen from the Mondays only departure from Monument Lane and the Saturdays only return, the engine spent the week outstationed at Albion

No.206 – TIPTON AND BLOOMFIELD SHUNTING ENGINE – CLASS 2 FREIGHT ENGINE

	Arr	Dep		Arr	Dep
Mon Lane Shed		5.10am (MO) LE	Tipton Shed		2.15pm
Tipton	5.30am*	7.50am LE	Tipton Yard	2.20pm*	9.40pm
Bloomfield	7.55am*	9.30am LE	Tipton Shed	9.45pm and finish	
Tipton	9.35am*	1.10pm	Repeat shunting routine daily, leaving Tipton shed to begin shunting yard at 5.30am as shown opposite		
Tipton shed	1.15pm		Tipton		7.2pm (SO) LE
			Mon Lane Shed	7.33pm	

*shunt

This engine spent the week outstationed at Tipton